UDL Navigators in Higher Education:

A Field Guide

BY JODIE BLACK
AND ERIC J. MOORE

CAST SKINNY BOOKS

UNTIL LEARNING HAS NO LIMITS™

Bulk discounts available: For details, email publishing@cast.org or visit
www.castpublishing.org.

Library of Congress Control Number: 2019939675

Paperback ISBN 978-1-930583-45-0
Ebook ISBN 978-1-930583-46-7

Published by:
CAST Professional Publishing
an imprint of CAST, Inc.
Wakefield, Massachusetts, USA

SKINNY BOOKS® is a registered trademark of CAST, Inc.

Cover and interior design by Happenstance Type-O-Rama

Printed in the United States of America

Contents

About the Authors

Jodie Black is a teaching and learning specialist at Fleming College in Peterborough, Ontario, Canada. She has worked with higher education institutions across Canada to integrate Universal Design for Learning into curriculum development, professional learning, teaching and learning, and student services. She actively presents at conferences, conducts workshops, and coaches others in the field about shifting mindsets and integrating UDL into systems and practices. She holds a master of education in teaching, learning, and curriculum from the University of New Brunswick.

Eric J. Moore is a UDL and accessibility specialist at the University of Tennessee, Knoxville (UTK), where he helps guide UDL integration on campus. He collaborates on designing instruction, offers professional development and training, and develops materials to support UDL and accessibility practices at UTK. He also conducts a private consultancy through his consulting firm at innospire.org. Eric has taught in the United States, and abroad in Indonesia and South Korea, engaging students from middle school through higher education in a range of subjects, including literature, philosophy, and inclusive education. He holds a PhD in inclusive education from the University of Tennessee, Knoxville.

Preface

*"I'm not a teacher: only a fellow traveler of whom you asked
the way. I pointed ahead—ahead of myself as well as you."*
—GEORGE BERNARD SHAW

Greetings, UDL Navigator! Yes, you! If you are picking
up this book, whatever your official role is in your
higher education institution, you clearly have ambitions
to learn about and help implement Universal Design for
Learning (UDL). You want to build trusting professional
relationships and put learning variability and expertise
at the heart of your work in higher education. You want
to help others discover the transformative potential of
this research-based framework. That makes you a UDL
Navigator.

As you know, higher education is a landscape of varied opportunities, challenges, and partnerships to navigate. Like you, those who promote UDL as a means of
improving the quality of education for all learners are
innovators and change agents—people at the front of a
movement to make learning environments more equita-
ble and effective.

While there is a great deal of published material about
UDL in the K–12 context, the higher education stakeholders
need something else. The perspectives of learners, instructors, and institutions are different in postsecondary settings

than in K–12, so many of the lessons from K–12 UDL implementation do not transfer. The complex aspects of higher
education mandates, funding, research demands, and more
also contribute to this difference. As such, we UDL innovators in postsecondary settings need to help each other navigate, learn, and improve through the sharing of successes,
setbacks, resources, and experiences. This book—the third
in CAST's Skinny Books® series—offers that help.

In this book, our aim is to equip Navigators with the
basic knowledge they need to apply UDL to curriculum
design, and support the development of UDL systems in
higher education. Each organizational context is unique,
so we have tried to select themes that are transferable
across colleges and universities. Using these themes, you
can tailor the work to your organization's needs, culture,
and values. Jodie works at a community college system in
Canada and Eric works in a large high-research-output
university in the United States. Also, both of us have con-
sulted and collaborated with others who work in various
types of colleges and universities in diverse national and
international settings. So, we believe that the perspectives
we share here are broadly applicable to UDL Navigators
across the higher education world.

UDL Navigators approach their work both as learners
and as leaders. You are perpetually learning and using
what you learn to lead and influence systems change,
build relationships, and foster improvement throughout
your organization. As Meyer, Rose, and Gordon (2014) put
it: "In educational settings, the goal of developing expertise is shared by all participants: students, teachers, and
all of the personnel in the system itself. If everyone is
focused on developing expertise as a learner, the context
is suffused with great models. Continual improvement,

engagement and growth are available to and expected of everyone" (p. 22).

We hope this field guide is just a starting point for the amazing places you will take your UDL integration. This guide shares lessons *we* have learned, informed by practical perspectives from the field. You're not alone in navigating the joys and complexities of UDL integration in higher education. We're all in this together!

Introduction:

Common Themes in Higher Education

In order to be strategic about and effective with UDL integration in higher ed, Navigators need to know their context. Higher education is a collection of systems within systems, each with both unique and shared characteristics; your success with integrating UDL into those systems depends on your knowledge of the existing systems and relationships among them. Much of what has been written about UDL to this point focuses on K–12 education. As we know, the higher education context is different in important ways.

Recognizing and responding to common themes, opportunities, and challenges in higher education is important to your work as a UDL Navigator because UDL design and delivery is deeply contextual. You'll need to be prepared with a vision for what UDL can look like in your context in order to help others see value and recognize how their work supports systemic change through UDL principles and values.

While we recognize that there is variability and nuance in terms of values, conditions, and structures based on your specific higher education context, we also know that there are some key themes that hold true across institutions. Being an effective Navigator in higher education means being well-versed both in UDL and the common qualities of institutions of higher education. Here we present some themes that we find to be relevant in our work as UDL Navigators. By deepening your understanding of these themes and finding connections that are relevant in your context, you will build credibility as a Navigator.

1. Adult learners and adult learning Depending on the nature of your institution, the adult students you serve may represent a wide range of ages, experiences, needs, goals, and expectations. In addition to our students, our instructors, administration, and staff whom we are seeking to enlist and support as they integrate UDL are, in this context, also adult learners who bring their education, careers, expertise, and experience. Considering all of our stakeholders as adults will help frame conversations about UDL. Elements such as individual choice, meaningful challenges, career preparation, development of lifelong learning dispositions, and work/life balance may be especially important to our adult learners, including students, instructors, and staff.

 SMART TIP Consider how the principles of UDL (provide multiple means of engagement, representation, and action and expression) correspond with the unique needs and barriers of adult learners. Making UDL connect, not compete, with adult learning principles can facilitate meaningful discussions into why and how UDL principles are effective for supporting adult learning.

2. Recruitment, retention, and persistence Recruitment and retention of students is an expensive endeavor for higher education institutions. Since students have so many choices, schools compete to attract and keep them in programs. Statistics like application funnels, program-specific retention, and persistence rates matter to administrators and instructors. They can determine program viability, student success data, and more. Being familiar with these terms and how that data is collected and used at your school is important.

 SMART TIP Consider starting your work by looking for courses or programs with low retention. How could a UDL approach help solve that problem? Schedule a meeting with department or program administrators and discuss how UDL implementation can improve retention rates. Think about recruitment from a UDL lens too. How could the recruitment process, often the first touchstone for potential students, design for variability?

3. Distinct graduate profiles A graduate profile is a vision for professional, cognitive, personal, and interpersonal competencies and skills that a student will have upon completion of a program. While the graduate profiles for high school students may look quite similar, graduate profiles of higher education students will differ significantly depending on program. For example, the graduate profile for students in a bachelor of engineering program will differ from students in a massage therapy diploma program. On the other hand, some programs that are quite different may share common aspects in their graduate profiles. For example, in Ontario there are Essential Employability Skills that align with many postsecondary programs in the province. Instructors are invested in the graduate profile for their program and in meeting the industry needs or community/field reputation of their program. Understanding the graduate profile for the institution as a whole and the specific nuances of the program in which instructors work will allow you to customize the message and approach that you take with UDL.

 SMART TIP   Think through how the graduate profile forms the "goal" of a whole program, and consider how UDL may be used to enhance that program or solve an existing problem for graduates who meet the profile. How could developing more learning expertise be a goal of the graduate profile?

4. External accreditation   Many programs are directly connected with professional bodies that are external to the higher education organization and have their own registrations and accreditation processes. Graduates of a program like nursing may have their credential of bachelor of nursing sciences, but must complete a registration test before they can practice in the field. In addition to that, most programs must be accredited by external licensing bodies to ensure the program is meeting the industry standard and to endorse graduates.

 SMART TIP   Find out what programs at your school have external accreditation. Learn the language and be intentional in showing where UDL can help enhance the program while still meeting accreditation standards and preparing students for an (often) standardized licensing-exam process. Be aware that sometimes the need to prepare students for external assessment is presented as a roadblock to innovation, and it's important to be cognizant of how faculty may perceive UDL as out of touch with realities of accreditation and standardized tests in the field.

5. Instructor autonomy, priorities, and curriculum control   In many higher education organizations, instructors have a lot of discretion over their time, academic priorities, and curriculum. However, they also have a lot to manage, including teaching, research, mentoring, industry connections, and committee work. As industry and subject experts, instructors often have significant influence over curriculum development, goals, methods, materials, and assessments. And while they may bring great industry or content expertise to those curricular choices, they may have varying levels of curriculum expertise. This offers opportunities for UDL Navigators to position UDL as a helpful curriculum design resource. Knowing the strengths and needs of your instructors will help you help them identify what design changes they want to make to improve their curriculum, teaching, and learning.

SMART TIP   Consider how to be strategic in recognizing the many roles that faculty play, when opportunities come up for significant curriculum revision, and when minor modifications are all that is reasonable. Show them how UDL can scale to make improvements iteratively at different stages in the curriculum lifecycle. We want integration of a UDL approach to be an engaging challenge, not an insurmountable threat!

6. Instructor Demographics   Instructors in higher education are variable. It is common in any institution to find a mix of faculty who are full-time and part-time; tenure track, lecturers, and adjuncts; and full professionals and graduate assistants. This means that students will take classes taught by instructors who will vary in their connection to the institution, opportunity for support, time commitment, capacity for influence, and control over curriculum (to name a few). Being aware of this dynamic is important to you, the UDL Navigator, because you need to be in tune with instructors' experience, including the realities of being part-time, adjunct, or a graduate assistant. For example, full-time instructors may have more involvement with program level curriculum development, and have community connections, while those who are part-time may exclusively be focused on the important work of effective course-level instruction. You'll need to think about how to build capacity; just like we want to reach all learners, we want to reach all instructors.

 SMART TIP   Consider the opportunities, constraints, and barriers for individual instructors with whom you work. Think about how UDL principles can be used and integrated iteratively without overwhelming faculty.

7. Instructors may not be trained to instruct   Unlike K–12 where most teachers have some undergraduate or graduate training in teaching and learning, higher education instructors have a much more varied professional lens and identity. Instructors will have expertise in their field or discipline or profession but may or may not have formal training in teaching and learning. They may teach from their own learning experiences or what modes they find more comfortable instead of integrating intentional learning-centered practices. This may impact their professional lens. Many instructors arrive with—or develop—teaching strategies and/ or work to intentionally hone their craft over time, so avoid assuming that they don't understand good pedagogical theory and practice. On the other hand, do not assume that because an instructor has been teaching a long time, they are an intentional teacher. The common ground is everyone has room to grow.

 SMART TIP   Plain language, analogies, stories, and clear examples go a lot further with some of our faculty than pedagogical theory and paradigms. Having a plain-language approach to practice with examples that are relevant in the field will be of huge benefit to you as a UDL Navigator.

8. Culture of teaching and learning   Every college or university—and often each program or department—has its own culture of teaching and learning; understanding that culture is critical for a UDL Navigator. Identifying where teaching and learning ranks on the institutional or departmental priority list will help you plan your approach. If other priorities, such as finance, expansion, instructor retention, key performance indicators (KPIs), program development, diversity, athletics, and/or research are a higher priority, that will give you valuable insight into the worlds of the instructors, staff, and administrators with whom you work. You can frame UDL as a way to help instructors solve their problems and meet their priorities. If you are lucky enough to work at a school where teaching and learning is the number one priority, you can still use this strategy.

 SMART TIP   Connect UDL with other curriculum frameworks and professional learning supports to enhance buy-in (you'll find examples of that in this Skinny book!). For a creative Navigator, learning about the current state is a critical step—assume nothing! Use existing and recognized priorities and challenges to frame initial discussions with stakeholders.

9. Academic and strategic plans and policies   Strategic and academic plans are the roadmaps for most higher education institutions. Maybe your school has different types of strategic planning documents that are especially influential with your teams. These may exist at multiple levels (e.g., university, college, or department). Get to know these documents and how UDL can connect to support or enhance these priorities. Seek out evidence to support your rationale. Even readily available information like key performance indicators, institutional research data, or even student surveys can be helpful when making rationales for how UDL can help reach strategic objectives. It's important for UDL not to operate outside of the system that it's trying to change, and as a Navigator you need to know the strategic directions of the school. If your school does not have a current strategic plan, get organized and ready to be part of the planning. Help others see how UDL helps them meet their strategic priorities. Get in there and make those connections!

 SMART TIP   Use existing strategies, missions, and visions as touchpoints when supporting a department or college with UDL integration. Explore opportunities for how UDL can help specifically support progress toward their existing goals or align with their existing strategic plan.

10. External legal and legislative requirements   In your jurisdiction, there will be various external requirements that must be met by your school and the people in it. These can include legal requirements, such as safety and accessibility; legislative requirements, such as Ministry, state/provincial, or national guidelines and spending protocols; or memoranda of understanding (MOUs) and board requirements. Knowing the external requirements that need to be met is helpful for a UDL Navigator. In our experience, legislation concerning accessibility and human rights is particularly important to know and a great "entry point" for UDL conversations. Although we know that UDL goes beyond accessibility, it can be an important way to initially build partnerships.

SMART TIP   Talk to administrators about what external requirements and obligations are important in the context in which you're working. Look for ways to use UDL to effectively and efficiently address those requirements while also enhancing teaching and learning. Be ready to discuss the intersections and distinctions between UDL and accessibility. Partner with the accessibility and human rights teams on campus to bring those important perspectives without convoluting UDL.

1

UDL and Program-Level Design

Intentionally designing engaging, inclusive learning experiences to develop expert learners is the focus of UDL educators and of UDL. In higher education, these learning experiences are usually packaged into programs, courses, and lessons and collectively called *the curriculum*. From a design perspective, we'll divide the discussion of curriculum into two separate but interconnected levels—the program level and the course level.

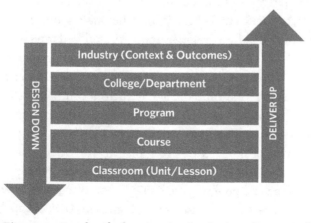

Figure 1.1. Levels of planning in developing the curriculum (Adapted frrom Olivia & Gordon, 2013, p. 39)

In this chapter, we are focusing on the integrated, program-level design that happens before a course even gets to the classroom and how you can layer UDL into that design.

Why It Matters

Intentional, program-level curriculum design enhances the opportunities for meaningful, engaging learning experiences. Many program-level aspects to curriculum development, like sequencing, assessment mapping, course types, and program-level outcomes, have opportunities to intentionally layer a UDL approach. Whatever curriculum frameworks or processes you or your colleagues use for program curriculum design, Universal Design for Learning can be layered in to add value throughout the processes. Infusing UDL from the program level will help ensure capacity for more effective design and instruction at the course level (remember, *design down, deliver up*?). To influence curriculum design, a UDL Navigator needs to be well aware of the dynamics of curriculum development in their institution.

One of the most important dynamics about program-level curriculum design is in who makes decisions. Programs are often driven by industry standards and economic needs and are determined or strongly influenced by accreditation bodies and program administrators. Because of these external influences, instructors can have relatively less influence over program-level curriculum, as opposed to course-level curriculum. This can be especially true of non-tenure-track instructors. Understanding the program-level curriculum processes and dynamics at your school give you credibility when discussing how UDL can be applied and identifying where UDL-aligned practices (perhaps not intentionally) are already happening. For example, it may be off-putting or simply ineffective to stress curriculum reform with an instructor who has little or no influence on program-level decisions. On the other hand, knowing how and why UDL can and should influence curriculum may be critical for conversations with relevant administrators, curriculum developers, or instructors preparing to provide voice in curriculum revision discussions.

Getting Our Bearings

As a UDL Navigator, you may or may not be positioned to influence curriculum right away. While we are taking a "top down" approach to examining curriculum and lesson design in this book, UDL Navigators often pragmatically will need to work more "bottom up," by working first with individual instructors, forming communities of practice and supporting transitions of learning design across departments and programs before gaining opportunity for influencing curriculum redesign. Nevertheless, you should think through how UDL may influence curriculum design and be prepared when opportunities arise.

To be effective at layering UDL into the curriculum design processes at your institution, first consider the curricular context. By curricular context, we mean both the processes and products of curriculum development. This includes the planning process for multiple levels of curriculum development, including the classroom, course, program, department, and industry levels, and any other inputs that feed into the outcomes, standards, assessments, and/or objectives to be covered in program courses.

In most postsecondary institutions, program-level curriculum is dynamic, often with regularly planned reviews and changes. The pace of curriculum change may differ from college to college and department to department. For example, industries that are rapidly evolving (e.g., computer science or education) may require more rapid curriculum changes than more stable industries (e.g., literature or philosophy). This reality provides potential opportunities for revisions using the principles and practices of UDL. How might a UDL Navigator support such revisions?

Taking Action: UDL and the Curriculum Design Process

Influencing program-level curriculum design requires UDL navigators to know the right questions to ask. To help, we've developed a set of relevant questions based on the 10 axioms of curriculum development created by Olivia and Gordon (2013). The axioms "offer guidelines that establish a frame of reference for workers seeking ways of operating and resolving problems. Several generally accepted axioms that apply to the curriculum field may serve to guide effectors that curriculum workers make for the purpose of improving the curriculum." (p. 22). We encourage you to reflect on these and discuss with your teams which might be the most important, contentious, ignored, or emerging at your schools.

As a UDL Navigator, you'll want to focus attention on the elements that may provide the clearest pathways to your involvement or influence in curriculum development. Broadly, these axioms address relationships among *people*, *context*, and *curriculum*. Because these three are always and inexorably related, when one changes, the others must also change. Change may begin with any of these three elements; based on where change begins, the process of responding may be different. Consider using the corresponding questions to prepare yourself and/or to facilitate discussion among other curriculum design stakeholders.

Table 1.1. Axioms of curriculum

	Axiom of curriculum (Olivia & Gordon, 2013, p 22–32)	UDL-informed questions for curriculum axioms
Change & Development	Change is both inevitable and necessary, for it is through change that life forms grow and develop.	▸ What is the change cycle for curriculum at my school? ▸ Who or what drives change (e.g., a regular review cycle or an indicator like poor enrollment)? ▸ How are students involved in curriculum review and development?
Curriculum & Context	A school curriculum not only reflects but also is a product of its time.	▸ How does this curriculum proactively plan for student learning? ▸ What outdated ideas about learning are used? (Watch for "learning styles" and other unproven clichés about how people learn.) ▸ How can you help the developers understand and integrate updated ideas about learning?
Curricular Legacy	Curriculum changes made at an earlier period of time can exist concurrently with newer curriculum changes at a later period of time.	▸ How can I support curriculum teams to make improvements without throwing out everything? ▸ How can I reduce the threat that UDL means that everything needs to be changed at once?

	Axiom of curriculum (Olivia & Gordon, 2013, p 22–32)	UDL-informed questions for curriculum axioms
Curriculum & Stakeholders	Curriculum change results from changes in people.	▸ How can I help the development team learn about learning variability and UDL? ▸ What are they already doing that aligns with a UDL approach? ▸ What are they doing that's a near miss (i.e., "learning styles" which is well-intentioned, but needs to be updated with current information about learning)?
Curriculum & Community	Curriculum change is affected as a result of cooperative endeavor on the part of groups.	▸ Who else can be involved in curriculum conversations? ▸ How can student services teams like accessibility services or international student services be involved? This may be particularly helpful at the learner analysis stage. ▸ How can student stakeholders or alumni be involved in curriculum development?
Curriculum & Decision Making	Curriculum development is basically a decision-making process.	▸ Who is making the decisions about what and how to teach? ▸ What external regulations influence those decisions? ▸ What is within the control of the curriculum development team? What is outside of its control?

	Axiom of curriculum (Olivia & Gordon, 2013, p 22–32)	UDL-informed questions for curriculum axioms
Perpetual Process	Curriculum development is a never-ending process	▸ How can I emphasize iterative improvements and small changes for UDL? ▸ How is curriculum quality evaluated? How can UDL indicators be layered into that evaluation?
Data and Information for Curriculum Change	Curriculum development is a comprehensive process.	▸ How can curriculum teams access demographic data or information about student learners? ▸ What data or information exists that help demonstrate a need for UDL? ▸ How will you measure curriculum improvements?
Systemic Change	Systematic curriculum development is more effective than trial and error.	▸ What program-level curriculum processes already exist for new program development and program review? ▸ How can I help systematize a UDL approach for curriculum teams through resources, processes, and so on?
Multiple Perspectives	The curriculum planner starts from where the curriculum is, just as the teacher starts from where the students are.	▸ How can I provide multiple entry points and possible starting points for UDL integration? One size will not fit all. ▸ How can I ensure that my approach to working with instructors and curriculum models UDL with our highly variable instructor learners?

Pulling It Together

In this chapter, we examined how UDL Navigators need to bridge the curriculum development and UDL worlds to be credible contributors to the program-level curriculum-development process. Whatever process your institution uses, the UDL framework and Guidelines can be used to begin thinking about how to affect change and improvement in course, assessment, lesson, or material design. UDL approaches need to be embedded and not work outside of existing processes. Likewise, UDL Navigators should seek to work synergistically with other stakeholders to accomplish collective goals, rather than trying to impose a standalone "UDL agenda."

When we get into the trenches of curriculum development, the amount of work that needs to be done can seem overwhelming. One of the most challenging aspects of practicing UDL is making reasonable improvements while accepting that everything cannot change at once. This also may be challenging for your instructor curriculum partners who, as they get excited, will be tempted to change it all at once! Remember that you needn't overhaul an entire course or program in one iteration. Curriculum development and UDL integration are both ongoing, collaborative processes.

Many instructors have found success by utilizing UDL design to improve one unit or one assessment to begin with and added further developments over time, based on new insights and student feedback. As many of us have experienced, it can take about three iterations to get a course to feel that it is as we want it to be. UDL implementation is similarly a back-and-forth process. Expect it to take a few runs to bring it to full implementation. Be sure to share successes and document those into the process. Early successes can motivate later efforts until whole courses, programs, departments, and colleges are influenced, sometimes because of the work of a single Navigator.

 PAUSE AND THINK

- How can students be involved in the curriculum design process?

- At your organization, what barriers do instructors need to overcome to make using such a design process work?

- What are current curriculum development processes at your school? How could you layer a UDL approach into those processes? How could UDL start to transform/enhance those processes?

- How can the goal of expert learners be infused in program-level outcomes?

- How can course sequencing support scaffolding and executive functioning?

- How can you support students who are unfamiliar with the more dynamic nature of UDL-oriented learning experiences?

Key Takeaways

▫ Program-level curriculum design is an important opportunity to integrate UDL.

▫ Understand your program development processes, then layer UDL into it to improve.

▫ Deepening your understanding of program-level curriculum design, such as learning the 10 axioms, will help you gain credibility and find opportunities to meaningfully layer UDL.

▫ Curriculum is about people—build those relationships!

2

UDL and Course-Level Design

In the previous chapter, we focused on how UDL can inform and transform program-level curriculum design, but what about courses? UDL can layer into course-level curriculum design, sometimes referred to at this stage as *learning design,* and this is often a place where most instructors have input and ideas to make course design come to life. When designing courses, we can layer in UDL to intentionally design engaging learning experiences for all students.

Why It Matters

Course design brings the program vision together with the day-to-day instruction. It is the most familiar package for instructors and students and an excellent area for UDL integration. UDL provides a powerful design framework *and* a well-structured set of research-based guidelines to help facilitate effective design and enable all learners to accomplish challenging learning outcomes while also developing as expert learners.

Course design is one area over which you, as a UDL Navigator, are likely to have a good deal of influence. UDL initiatives in higher education often begin with learning experience design for individual instructors, which becomes a small group that keeps on growing. This is an area with near immediate impact on student performance, and thus offers potential for great anecdotal evidence or action research. When we get this right, other opportunities follow.

Getting Our Bearings

Course design is usually led by instructors, and when we Navigators present UDL to instructors during course design, we need to be thoughtful about how we present it. Our instructors are learners, too, and you want to engage them with clear goals and multiple means of engagement, representation, and action and expression. We like to draw attention to UDL as a design framework that intentionally draws from research to enhance learning for everyone. Framing the UDL approach in terms of the design frame rather than leading with the UDL Guidelines is important. When we have led with the Guidelines, we've often seen two problematic reactions. Sometimes instructors balk at the sight of 31 checkpoints under nine Guidelines and three principles. They may feel overwhelmed by the misconception that they need to practice all of these in their lesson design all the time. Alternatively, instructors may pick out some best practices from the Guidelines that look familiar or that they have practiced and determine that "UDL is nothing new" or suggest that they are *already* doing UDL. This type of resistance does happen sometimes, but don't get discouraged! It means you need to find another way to connect and engage.

The Guidelines are wonderful and very important to the practice of UDL, but only when they are used as part of the intentional design process. That process is, therefore, the better place to start. In the following section, we'll examine both the design process and the Guidelines and how you can use the two conjointly to support the design and development of learning experiences for everyone.

Rose, Meyer, and Gordon (2014) provide a UDL-informed approach to designing curriculum through an intentional design of goals, assessments, methods, and materials. In this way, a UDL approach can be layered into various design approaches and allows for flexibility across multiple approaches. By knowing and applying this perspective to multiple processes, you can be flexible to the needs and directions of the people you're working with and layer a UDL approach. In Table 2.1, we align Meyer, Rose, and Gordon's (2014) UDL perspective on goals, assessments, methods, and materials with some questions that might help facilitate the conversation by linking course design to UDL.

Focusing on goals, assessments, methods, and materials can apply to any learning design process. We challenge you to think of the learning design processes you know and use and find ways to layer a UDL approach. We'll show you two examples in the next section. Whatever process you use, making sure that goals, assessments, methods, and materials align is critical.

Table 2.1. Areas of course design and corresponding UDL design questions

Area	Considerations	Opening questions
Goals	Separate the means from the end	▶ What must students do to achieve this goal? ▶ What is the process or the product for this learning outcome? ▶ How would you assess mastery for that goal?
	Consider all three learning networks	▶ Are there goals that include learning expertise? ▶ What goals are included for self-assessment and reflection? Applying knowledge to new situations? Self-regulation and strategy development?
	Challenge all learners	▶ How will these goals challenge (not threaten) your learners? ▶ What steps might be needed to ensure challenge is maintained?
	Actively involve learners	▶ How can students be a part of creating goals or mini-goals?
Assessments	Are ongoing and focused on learner progress	▶ How are the assessments structured? ▶ Are there summative and formative assessments?
	Measure both product and process	▶ Are there assessments providing mastery-oriented feedback? ▶ Are there grades awarded?
	Are flexible, not fixed	▶ Are there choices where possible? ▶ What can flexibility look like in this assessment?

Area	Considerations	Opening questions
Assessments (cont.)	Are construct relevant	► Are the assessments measuring what they're intending to measure? ► Do they align to the learning goals?
	Actively inform and involve learners	► How will learners know about the criteria for success in the assessment? ► How can learners be involved in the assessing process (i.e., establishing goals or criteria or providing feedback)?
Methods	Can be continually adjusted to meet learner needs	► How do you go beyond your comfort zone when teaching? ► How do you or could you match methods with goals?
	Include all students within a collaborative environment	► How do you build classroom community and collaboration? ► How do you define collaboration? ► How do your students define collaboration?
Materials	Align to goals	► What materials would help learners reach that learning goal?
	Engage all learners in becoming proactive	► How can materials help students to measure their progress and collaborate over time?

Taking Action: Layering UDL and Course Design

Every institution will have a different course design process, but we know that UDL can layer onto any process, so we wanted to share two examples of course-level design processes that are frequently used: Wiggins and McTighe's backward design and the instructional design process, ADDIE. We chose to use these as examples because UDL can layer into different design approaches with many different types of learning experiences and intended outcomes. We want to show how you can layer UDL to improve course-level design regardless of the framework.

Backward Design

In its basic form, the Wiggins and McTighe backward design process focuses design of learning experiences on three broad steps: establish clear outcomes, design assessments, and design the instructional experience. Once the design is completed, skilled instructors follow through with intentional delivery and reflection. Figure 2.1 shows these three broad steps.

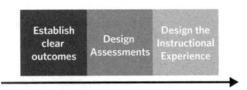

Figure 2.1: Three broad steps of backward design

The backward design approach to designing may be new in some higher education contexts, wherein it is common for instructors to begin course design by choosing a textbook and using it to drive what content they deliver. The primary strength of the backward design framework is that it encourages educators to define a clear outcome and to use the intended outcome to make all other decisions about learning and teaching. Backward design is also transferable to learning design at the classroom, course, or program level. How can you layer UDL onto a backward design process? First, intentionally plan for learner variability (Figure 2.2). Second, apply the UDL framework to inform the entire design process, including goals, assessments, instructional experience, and reflection.

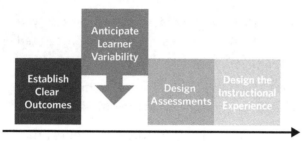

Figure 2.2. Adding anticipation of learner variability into the backward design frame.

Let's start with adding the important step of anticipating learner variability to the backward design process. When using backward design, you start with a clear outcome or goal, and then choose assessments, methods, and materials that will best enable learners to achieve the intended outcomes. But who are our learners? Without considering what we've learned in recent years about the variability of learners in terms of the affective, recognition, and strategic networks of the brain, backward design may be used to create lessons that are highly focused in terms of content, but still ineffective for individual learners. We can design high-quality content with backward design but still be frustrated when students do not engage in the learning, comprehend the information, or successfully express themselves in assessments. That's why we need to anticipate learner variability.

PAUSE AND THINK

□ Which design processes does your institution use? How would you layer UDL into that process?

□ What UDL-informed design processes do you prefer? Backward design? ADDIE? Integrated design? Something else? Why?

□ How would you respond to instructors who feel like designing with UDL is too time-intensive?

□ How would you help instructors identify priorities for redesign? How would the UDL framework help inform that decision-making?

Second, the UDL Guidelines and the goal of expert learning can be used to inform all steps in the backward design process. This is shown visually in Figure 2.3. For example, in *establishing clear outcomes*, the UDL Guidelines advocates for a goal of developing expert learners; that is, learners who are "purposeful and motivated, resourceful and knowledgeable, and strategic and goal-directed." This may seem above and beyond a specific content goal, but could be something instructors add as a "learner profile" objective, especially if it was specific to the course and content. To this end, the newest version of the Guidelines graphic organizer also clarifies how the Guidelines are organized horizontally, moving from "access" to "build," to "internalize" levels as practices move toward learner independence. Further, the principle "provide multiple means of engagement" provides guidance in formulating goals that are salient, relevant, and engaging.

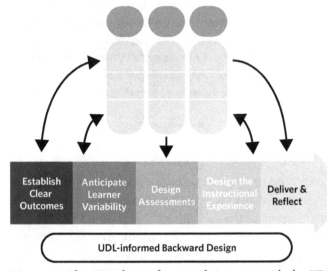

Figure 2.3. The UDL design framework interacts with the UDL Guidelines throughout.

Likewise, the Guidelines are useful to inform the *anticipate learner variability* step in the process. While it may be challenging to brainstorm all the ways students may be predictably variable, the checkpoints may provide ideas about the variability that the Guidelines anticipate. For example, "activate or supply background knowledge" may help consider how students vary in terms of what they know coming into a course or lesson.

SMART TIP Don't lose sight of accessibility!
Keeping accessibility in UDL without perpetuating
the myth that UDL is only about accessibility or exclusively to help students with disabilities is important.
We like to emphasize that the first row of the UDL
Guidelines aligns to improving access for all, but the
framework doesn't stop there! UDL is about helping all
learners achieve not only access but also to become
expert learners. Keep accessibility in the design, keep
moving through the other rows of the UDL framework,
and keep moving towards expert learning!

The UDL framework can also be used to inform the
design and development of assessments, and the instructional experience, including methods, and materials. The
organization of the Guidelines is very useful for this purpose because of the logical way the UDL framework is
organized. We can point out to instructors how the UDL
Guidelines provide us with a way to "chunk" these practices according to the nine Guidelines, three major learning
networks, and corresponding principles. This presentation
enables many meaningful usages, including the capacity
to think about learning issues that students are encounter-
ing because of the environment and then thinking through
corresponding Guidelines and checkpoints to brainstorm
solutions by design. For example, if students are losing
focus in class, ask "What would help? How can I clarify the
learning goal then design with more options for expression,
action and engagement, and representation?"

In these ways, UDL is best implemented throughout a design process in which the Guidelines influence

decisions in each step. Layering UDL onto backward design is a useful place to start, especially if your instructors are already working with backward design.

UDL and the ADDIE Model of Instructional Design

UDL can also layer onto the widely used ADDIE model of instructional design (which stands for analysis, design, develop, implement, and evaluate). ADDIE provides a series of steps to guide the course design process and we've layered UDL-informed questions on each step. Again, regardless of the specific course design process we're using, we focus on (1) intentional planning for learner variability and (2) a UDL-informed approach to decision-making and design. In Table 2.2, we provide several examples that you may use to prepare for conversations and/or to facilitate conversation around the role of UDL in ADDIE steps. These questions are informed by learner variability, the UDL principles, and a UDL perspective on goals, assessments, methods, and materials.

Table 2.2. ADDIE steps and corresponding UDL-informed questions

ADDIE Steps	UDL Informed Questions
Analysis	▸ How can learning variability be used in the analysis of learners? ▸ How can a UDL approach be used to inform goal-setting? ▸ What implied learning goals could be made explicit? ▸ What prior knowledge or skills will learners need to participate in this course? ▸ How has accessibility been planned for in the online and physical environments?

ADDIE Steps	UDL Informed Questions
Design	▸ What's the approach to design? ▸ Have multiple representations been considered when planning media and materials? ▸ Are there goals that align with expert learning? ▸ Are the goals scaffolded to support progress? ▸ How are prototypes being measured? ▸ How is executive functioning being planned for and supported? ▸ How are formative assessments used to provide mastery-oriented feedback in addition to content-based feedback?
Development	▸ Are a variety of learners, including those who use assistive technologies, asked to provide feedback during development and testing? ▸ Are a variety of materials and assessments being used?
Implementation	▸ How are learners and teachers being supported? ▸ What adjustments are being made during the roll out of the design?
Evaluation	▸ Are key UDL concerns such as expert learning, motivation, mastery, and accessibility addressed by the evaluation?

UDL and Integrated Course Design

Our last example of layering UDL with existing course design processes is with Dee Fink's Integrated Course Design. Although a UDL approach layers onto many aspects of Integrated Course Design, we wanted to highlight the connections to the alignment of primary components. The alignment of teaching and learning activities, feedback and assessment, and learning goals provides a clear foundation for a UDL approach. With the acknowledgment that situational factors play an important part in what's possible in design, instructors often appreciate the pragmatism of this approach.

In the initial design phase, Fink provides prompts for course design conversations. We've layered some additional UDL prompts to each section so you can mix and match UDL and Fink in Table 2.3.

Table 2.3. Integrating a UDL approach to Fink's (2003) Integrated Course Design

Fink's Initial Design Phase	Fink's Existing Prompts	Additional UDL Approach Prompts
1. Careful consideration of situational factors	▸ What is the special instructional challenge of this particular course? ▸ What is expected of the course by students, the department, the institution, the profession, and society at large? ▸ How does this course fit into the larger curricular context?	▸ What do we know about learning and learning variability? How can we plan for it in this program? ▸ Is our goal to improve access, instruction, or learning expertise with our students? ▸ How can a UDL-informed approach help us with our design process? ▸ What barriers (i.e., physical, sensory, cognitive, informational, technological, social, linguistic, affective, attitudinal) exist in the program? ▸ What do the instructor subject matter experts need to learn about curriculum development and learning to make them more effective?

Fink's Initial Design Phase	Fink's Existing Prompts	Additional UDL Approach Prompts
2. Learning goals	▸ What do you want students to learn by the end of the course, that will still be with them several years later? ▸ Think expansively, beyond "understand and remember" kinds of learning. ▸ Suggestion: Use the taxonomy of "Significant Learning" as a framework.	▸ What might get in the way of our diverse learners reaching these learning goals? ▸ Do these goals separate the means from the end of the goal? This will allow more options for assessment without lowering standards. ▸ If learning expertise is a curricular goal, how do these learning goals support students developing expertise?
3. Feedback and assessment procedures	▸ What will the students have to do, to demonstrate that they have achieved the learning goals (as identified above)? ▸ Think about what you can do that will help students learn, as well as give you a basis for issuing a course grade.	▸ Do assessments have construct-irrelevant features that could be eliminated? ▸ How will students self-assess and measure their progress? ▸ How will formative feedback be used to support student learning? ▸ How will students understand and interpret the instructor's expectations for evaluative assessment?

Fink's Initial Design Phase	Fink's Existing Prompts	Additional UDL Approach Prompts
4. Teaching and learning activities	▸ What would have to happen during the course for students to do well on the feedback and assessment activities? ▸ Think of creative ways of involving students that will support your more expansive learning goals. ▸ Suggestion: Use "Active Learning" activities, especially those related to "Rich Learning Experiences" in which students achieve several kinds of significant learning. Simultaneously look for "In-depth Reflective Dialogue" opportunities for students to think and reflect on what they are learning, how they are learning, and the significance of what they are learning.	▸ How will you ensure learning materials are accessible by design? This includes video, audio, text, web conferencing, textbooks, open educational resources, and learning management systems. ▸ How will you use technology to increase multiple means of engagement, representation, and action and expression? ▸ How will the teaching and learning activities support strategy development and critical thinking? ▸ What activities might have unintentional barriers for students? Think about field trips, labs, simulations, group work, online learning, and so on. Are these activities construct-relevant or construct-irrelevant? ▸ What could be solved through designing with more learners in mind?

Fink's Initial Design Phase	Fink's Existing Prompts	Additional UDL Approach Prompts
5. Make sure the key components are integrated	▸ Check to ensure that the key components (Steps 1-4) are all consistent with and support each other	▸ How will graduated levels of progress be woven throughout the program/course? ▸ Do the goals, assessments, methods, materials align? ▸ How have you intentionally planned for learning variability? How has the development team developed their understanding of learning variability?

Pulling It Together

Intentionally designed program- and course-level curriculum provides the foundation for all learners to access and engage with meaningful learning experiences. As UDL Navigators, we know that effective learning experiences don't happen by accident and are always looking for ways to bring UDL into the conversation for both program- and course-level design. Be prepared to layer UDL on different processes such as backward design, ADDIE, or Integrated Course Design as a streamlined way of introducing UDL and the UDL Guidelines to identify and address barriers at the design stage. UDL doesn't need to compete with existing design approaches; it can complement and enhance approaches to improve the design experience for all.

When designing or redesigning, remember that change does not happen overnight. Many instructors have found success by utilizing UDL design to improve one unit or one assessment to start with, and then iteratively added further developments over time based on new insights and student feedback. As many of us have experienced, it can take about three iterations to get a course to feel that it is as we want it to be; UDL implementation in a course is the same. Expect it to take a few runs to bring it to full implementation. Be sure to share successes and document those into the process. Early successes can motivate later efforts, until whole courses, programs, departments, and colleges are influenced, sometimes because of the work of a single Navigator.

Key Takeaways

▫ Course design is an important opportunity to layer UDL.

▫ Build relationships and trust with instructors to create the foundations for curriculum partnerships.

▫ Learn your organization's course design context before layering UDL.

▫ UDL can layer in to improve any course design process by adding intentional planning for learning variability and development of learner expertise using the Guidelines.

▫ Like course design, integrating UDL is iterative and doesn't have to be perfect all at once!

3

UDL + Teaching and Learning

The teaching and learning experience takes the program- and course-level designs and brings them to life. This is where the instructor-student interactions begin, engagement is sparked, and adjustments are made. In this chapter, we'll explore how UDL can inform instructors' (and students'!) day-to-day work of teaching and learning.

Why It Matters

Teaching and learning is the heart of education. A thoughtfully designed curriculum is an important foundation and it comes alive with teachers and students engaging in motivating and purposeful learning experiences. In higher education, instructor attitudes and actions form one of the strongest institutional variables that influence student experience and retention and can have a powerful effect on learner outcomes (Elliott & Healy, 2001; Lundquist, Spalding, & Landrum, 2002; Shelton, 2003). Beyond the research, many of us can remember K–12 teachers, higher education instructors, or other types of teachers whose influence on our lives and our interest in the content had more to do with how they taught and how they made us feel than the curriculum. As David Rose, who coauthored the UDL framework, often said: "Teaching is emotional work."

Teaching experiences in higher education vary immensely in many ways, including the content being taught, the context of the school and classroom, the teaching experience of the instructor, the technology available, and more. Moreover, instruction occurs in various environments: in lecture halls, online via learning management systems, in lab spaces, on field trips, and in simulation rooms, tutorial spaces, and more. While it may look different depending on the context, accessible, engaging, effective teaching is possible across settings.

The teaching and learning experience is a main focus of UDL integration because it's the ultimate intersection of all instructional design. Just like the blueprint for a house cannot be lived in, quality instructional design must result in practical action to demonstrate value. For some, practicing one's plan is the most difficult step. Designing good instruction on paper is one thing, but converting that plan into action is another. This may be readily apparent if we think about simply handing a UDL lesson plan to an instructor who has never heard about UDL or been trained in inclusive praxis and expecting them to execute it as intended.

Further, during the design process, instructors may often enlist the support of instructional designers, curriculum specialists, or others to aid in the process. But executing instruction is often a solo act for instructors and relies on instructor efficacy and skill to convert well-designed plans into action. Instructors also commonly face barriers to delivering quality instruction in practice because of variability in their experience or preparation to teach, physical or digital spaces that may be far from ideal, and financial, time, and technological constraints. In light of these variable barriers, instructors need realistic, flexible supports to lift UDL from paper to practice. In this chapter, we'll explore how you as a Navigator, or you and your team, can work with instructors to integrate UDL into their teaching and experiences.

Getting Our Bearings

Applying UDL to the teaching and learning experience often means changing both thinking and practice. For instructors practicing UDL, there are multiple factors to consider. The biggest concerns that we hear are:

1. We don't have enough time to make these changes.

2. The space isn't accessible or flexible, so how can I implement UDL?

3. I don't want to lower the academic rigor.

4. I'm already doing this.

Instructor time and capacity is an important concern to address. It's true that instructors–like everyone–have limited time and resources. Space can seem like a fixed factor that's hard to change with old building and classroom timetables. Academic standards are important to learners' growth and program quality. Building on strengths and recognizing alignments matters, too, because no one likes to be told they're doing things wrong. You may have concerns that you would add to this list. Instructors have a lot of change coming at them, and UDL may seem like another "flavor of the month." As UDL Navigators, it's important for us to be ready to address concerns and use those to build trusting relationships with instructors. To help instructors, we have to discuss and address those concerns. One of the foundational skills we suggest will best support all these concerns is relationship-building. One concrete way we suggest that you support instructors is by helping them focus on practical things they can do soon, and helping them address and be intentional in the use of some of their time and resources for this purpose.

The UDL Guidelines are a good tool for doing this, because they address environmental barriers in challenging teaching spaces. As we present ideas for each domain, the point of this short chapter isn't to provide an exhaustive inventory of solutions, but to demonstrate that instructors *can* practice UDL in the lecture hall, a limited LMS, or other, more restrictive environments.

 SMART TIP   One way to engage instructors in a UDL approach is to start with what's not working for them and their students. Ask questions like, "If you could change one thing about this course, what would it be?" "What do students often complain about?" "What assignment do students have the most questions about?" By addressing existing problems, the UDL solution becomes more authentic because it is already grounded in the instructors' personal experiences.

Taking Action: Intentionally Layering UDL into Teaching and Learning

We reviewed how to layer UDL into the program- and course-level design processes in the previous chapters, and now we're going to narrow our focus to teaching and learning. While this is important for all instructors, this may be particularly useful for instructors looking for something more "in the moment" for their own teaching and learning dilemmas and things that are within their immediate control. Whatever they're teaching, you can help them. Two go-tos in our toolkit are:

- The UDL Guidelines, printed out, in color (udlguidelines.cast.org)
- A custom adaptation of the "4 Elements of Instruction" from the UDL-IRN (2011)
- A strengths-based attitude
- Problem-solving skills
- Active listening

We'll show you two ways that you might approach layering UDL with teaching and learning when working with instructors. Of course, feel free to mix and match.

Option 1: Start with the Barriers, Solve with the Guidelines.

Once instructors are engaged and motivated to convert UDL-designed curriculum to UDL praxis, the next thing is to very intentionally consider how UDL will work in the context of their physical or digital teaching and learning space(s). This means walking back over the Guidelines and drawing from the principles and checkpoints to maximize the strengths of each learning environment while mitigating its barriers. Let's consider some examples for each principle. Often, it works well to start with the student's experience, identify barriers in the learning environment (not the student!), and then brainstorm design strategies using the Guidelines. We'll go through some examples using each principle of the UDL framework.

Provide Multiple Means of Engagement

Every learning environment has some potential barriers to engagement, and we need to plan for them. For example, a prevailing attitude among students about general education classes taught in large lecture halls is that they can "get them out of the way"—a toxic attitude for learning. But simply ignoring such attitudes won't address the problem. Recruiting interest, sustaining effort, and promoting self-regulation among students is a challenge that everyone assigned to teach in the large lecture hall must face. In UDL, the first place we look to solve problems is the environment, not the student.

Similarly, online experiences may stifle engagement for many students who would come alive in person. (And vice versa! Students who may be disengaged in person may become avid contributors online.) Intentionally fostering a sense of community in the online environment and keeping lines of communication open among students and instructors to underscore expectations of interaction and engagement can be especially important in an online setting. Designing environments that have options for engagement lets more students engage in ways that optimize their own learning.

Consider the following sample strategies to make learning more engaging. Again, these suggestions aren't intended to be comprehensive or prescriptive. Our intent is to demonstrate the thought process for noticing student behaviors and experiences, identifying environmental barriers, considering checkpoints to address those barriers, and drawing from practices that will apply those checkpoints appropriately in context. Some of these will only be relevant in certain environments (e.g., lecture halls or asynchronous online settings), and others may be generally applicable.

Table 3.1. Designing for engagement.

Potential Student Experience	Common Barriers	Possible Design Strategy
Students are disengaged during the learning experience.	► Lecture segments are too long ► Not enough time to reflect and think. Too much one-way talking. ► Content is disconnected from their own experience	► "Flip" the lecture portion of a lesson (move it to being used outside of class), adding interactive elements and breaking it up into shorter segments. ► Provide students with opportunity to respond, reflect, and practice during the learning experience with backchannels, response systems, or simply think-pair-share opportunities. ► Draw from current events, use high-interest examples, or connect to student interests to make points in the learning experience.

Potential Student Experience	Common Barriers	Possible Design Strategy
Students are disinterested in the course/ content/topic from day one.	► Students aren't involved in creating the learning topics ► Topics chosen aren't relevant to the learners ► Course material or teaching approach is inauthentic to students	► Ask students why they signed up for the course or what they'd like to learn in it. Use those topics to inform the lessons. ► In the first class, choose a real-life, high-interest example that utilizes the subject matter at hand, and provide students with an opportunity to grapple with it individually or in groups. ► Openly talking about attitudes toward the course and encourage students to know that you do realize it and understand it and want to address it. Encourage them to talk to you about their ambitions and inhibitions related to the course.
Learners feel overwhelmed by information presented in lectures.	► No clear goals for the lessons or assignments ► Other than final grades, few opportunities for feedback are provided	► Set a clear, manageable, and reasonably challenging learning objective for each lesson. ► Provide students opportunity to check their progress toward that objective and to recognize their success. For example, use class response tools like clickers, provide self-check problems, or give a scenario before class and then again after and have students note how their understanding has changed.

Providing Multiple Means of Representation

Contemporary lectures tend to involve lots of verbal information with textual support in the form of a Power-Point projected on a main screen. This mode of lecture is so ubiquitous that many instructors find themselves using it without stopping to question: is this the most effective way to represent information? Is such a lecture the best use of precious class time with students?

The answer to both questions is almost uniformly no. For one thing, students with hearing and/or visual disabilities will struggle with this format and require accommodation support to manage. For learners who would benefit from more graphic representation or hands-on experience, the lecture-and-text format poses serious limitations for learning. For students who struggle with attending to extended speech, the requirements posed by this form of representation may make sustaining focus for a full hour exceedingly difficult. And so on. In fact, I am not sure I could possibly find students for whom lecture-and-text is the optimal representation format for learning. Yet, this is exactly the purpose for which large lecture halls are designed!

Consider the sample strategies in Table 3.2 to provide flexibility in representation.

Table 3.2. Designing for representation

Potential Student Experience	Common Barriers	Possible Design Strategy
Students struggle with text-based presentations.	▶ There are only text-based representations on slides. ▶ No preview option is available before class.	▶ If you use presentations, design them to be text-minimalist. Use short sentences for major points only, in larger font. Replace excess text with visual representations: graphs, pictures, or short videos. Keep the long blocks of texts for your notes. ▶ Make the presentation available to students on their own devices either live with the presentation (e.g., with Nearpod or Keynote Live) or independently (e.g., post a PDF version of the presentation to the course LMS before class). This will allow students to customize their own displays and take notes on their own devices as they attend the presentation.
Students have bad days, and sometimes need to miss class, and so on, and thus lose access to content taught in a given class day.	There's only one way to access synchronous class experiences	▶ Record class (seek student permission first) and enable students to access videos later, outside of class, for review or to catch up for necessary misses.

Potential Student Experience	Common Barriers	Possible Design Strategy
Learners vary in background knowledge (including language) and/or capacity to understand or recall key concepts and terms.	▸ Lots of new vocabulary that hasn't been defined ▸ Lessons don't connect and build on previous lessons. ▸ Lots of new material taught, but no way to practice with it and get immediate feedback	▸ Create a bank of these terms (which will grow over the length of the course) and share this with students prior to the lecture. Explain new words or symbols when you use them the first couple of times. ▸ Intentionally recall key prerequisite information at the start of lectures, so students have it fresh in their mind for the present. ▸ As a routine, during and/or at the end of each lecture, have students apply concepts to practical scenarios for the sake of conceptualization and transfer.

Providing Multiple Means of Action & Expression.

In some environments—like large lecture halls—attending class in a large lecture hall is intended to be something like attending a performance. Significant participation is neither expected nor facilitated. The primary action students are expected to take, in addition to listening, is to take good notes. This format maintains the focus on the instructor and the content and is not conducive to variability in student expressive needs or skill sets. On the contrary, many online instructors *want* their students to be actively involved and participating but struggle to facilitate meaningful interaction in the setting. Consider these sample strategies for how instructors may provide flexibility for student action and expression.

Table 3.3. Designing for action & expression

Potential Student Experience	Common Barriers	Possible Design Strategy
Some students struggle to listen in class and take notes at the same time.	Only one option for note taking. Every person for themselves!	▸ Explicitly teach and encourage collaborative note taking using cloud-based documents (e.g., Google Docs, Word Online). This reduces the pressure on individual students to catch everything and encourages them to take good notes as-and for-a team.
Some students feel awkward or shy speaking up in class, especially in a large class.	There are no options for asking questions.	▸ Make the use of a backchannel a central part of the class both during and after lectures to keep students in the conversation. Respond to them in real time, when appropriate, during the lecture. ▸ If lecture is needed, break it up into 10–15 minute stretches, followed by an opportunity for students to express themselves in different ways. For example, poll, ask questions, discuss with peers, practice a strategy, challenge a position, and so forth. ▸ Reserve the last 5–10 minutes of class for students to complete a prompted reflection journal regarding takeaways from the day's class and raise additional questions if they didn't get to ask. Follow up on these as warranted.
Some people struggle with sitting still and focusing for prolonged periods.	There's just one type of seating	▸ Create a space in the back of the room where students who need to stand up, stretch, or move around a little can freely do so without disturbing others or feeling awkward.

Potential Student Experience	Common Barriers	Possible Design Strategy
Some students find it difficult to maintain focus in synchronous online classes, when other tabs in their browser with chats and games and shopping are ever tempting.	The online learning environment invariably includes significant potential distractions.	▶ Be open and frank about the challenges of maintaining focus in online classes, talking about the importance of keeping only the class materials on screen. ▶ Give students opportunities to share and check in at regular intervals to "keep them honest" and reduce drifting. ▶ Provide breaks in long classes to enable some free time.

Option 2: Using a UDL Approach to Unit and Lesson Planning

We've created a mashup of "Four Elements of UDL Instruction" (https://udl-irn.org/home/udl-resources/) from the UDL-IRN's (2011) Instructional Planning Process and the "Four elements of UDL curriculum" (goals, methods, materials, assessments) from CAST to detail a synthesized approach of our own (See the sidebar "A Closer Look"). This generally linear and step-by-step approach gives greater clarity and structure for design than the UDL Guidelines do by themselves. For Navigators or instructors who prefer more structure, this is a pathway to help support integration of UDL into instructional design and is especially helpful for planning lessons and units. The steps are established clear and measurable goals, and allow instructors to intentionally consider and plan for learner variability.

A CLOSER LOOK   Go to https://
bit.ly/2UGovmV to read the critical
elements of UDL instruction.

*Establish Clear and Measurable Goals. Lessons and Units
Need Clear, Measurable Goals to Guide Learning and
Instructional Planning.*

In addition to setting clear, rigorous, content-based goals,
use a UDL approach to consider learning goals directly
related to the development of expert learners. The question becomes not just, "How can I support students in
learning chemistry?" but also, "How can I support my students in learning to self-regulate, identify tools to support
their learning, and develop their executive function skills?"
(See Fink, 2003 for more on this point). Another consider-
ation for lesson-based learning goals is mini-goals. How
can you break down the learning outcomes of the course
into smaller, lesson-sized steps to guide progress monitoring? For example, if the learning outcome is "Describe
how totalitarianism contributed to the first world war,"
you would need to break that down into smaller learning
goals. Those goals might be things like "Define totalitarianism," "Define democracy," and "Compare totalitarianism with democracy using your own examples." Use those
mini goals to guide the lesson planning.

Intentionally Consider and Plan for Learner Variability.

In general, it's safe to assume that instructors care about
their students and about the students' learning in their

programs. They are also using the Guidelines and research to help them understand the diversity they see in their students as learning variability is an important step. Often, dealing with the popular neuromyth of "learning styles" is an obstacle at this stage (Newton, 2015).

The Guidelines may also be used as a starting point to help facilitate the conceptual shift from learning styles to predictable variability both between and within learners based on context and content. In conversations with people who understand and value the learning styles neuromyth, consider explaining the ways that predictable variability enhances and more accurately represents learning and learners. For example, you may use these points of comparison:

- Where learning styles focuses on learning primarily in terms of how learners prefer to perceive and comprehend information, predictable variability recognizes the role of perception and comprehension for learning, but also stresses how important engagement and learner expression is to the process of learning.

- Where learning styles focuses on identifying the one way that individuals would learn something (e.g., audio, visual, hands-on), predictable variability does not assume such a static best method for learners but demonstrates that learners are different from context to context and moment to moment. Individuals learn best when provided with multiple or flexible options to choose from throughout the learning experience.

Use the Guidelines to jog thinking about the kind of variability we can anticipate in students and to frame the student characteristics they see in a learning frame. Help them move beyond simply thinking in terms of responding to disability to consider how learning variability can inform design. Things like communication (Guideline 5), motivation and persistence (Guidelines 7–8), or language or symbol decoding (Guideline 2) may be opportunities for enhanced design of the learning experience.

Plan Meaningful and Informative Assessments. Both Formative and Summative Assessments Need to Align with Your Clear Learning Course- and Lesson-Based Goals.

Often the first well-intentioned UDL tip that we want to provide is "provide flexibility and choices with assessments." This can be a threatening first move for instructors and appear to risk more work and compromised standards. Instead, here is a great place to offer choice and scaffolding. *Flexible assessments* does not refer exclusively to offering options for demonstrating mastery (e.g., choose among essay, presentation, or podcast). While that's one way to offer flexibility, it's not the only one. We like to think of flexibility in assessments as a continuum. While this continuum can apply to both formative and summative assessments, the formative options are on the left end of the continuum and the more summative options move to the right side. While offering options for assessment format may be valid and useful for assessing student understanding in general, instructors obviously cannot provide alternatives to writing an essay if writing the essay is the required outcome (e.g., in a composition course). Fortunately, there are fewer intensive ways of offering flexibility in such cases (Figure 3.1).

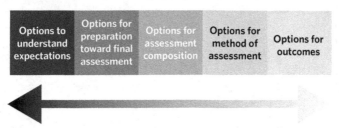

Figure 3.1. Continuum of ways to offer assessment flexibility

For example, if students need to write an essay to demonstrate specified outcomes, the two options to the far right are not feasible, but there are other ways to offer flexibility, such as offering options for composition (e.g., teaching more-vocal students to use speech-to-text to compose essays), options for preparations (e.g., showing students different ways to organize their ideas prior to writing), options for understanding expectations (e.g., rubrics, examples, and non-examples). On the other hand, in some situations, the assessment and even the outcome can be determined by the student (e.g., capstone projects). This approach can lower the threat of making significant changes to assessments and present some meaningful options for flexibility in both formative and summative assessments in the lesson and unit level.

Another approach to lesson- and unit-based assessments is layering a UDL approach to assessments. This may be a good learning opportunity for instructors who aren't familiar with best practices of assessment or can connect some of their approaches with good principles of assessment. Here we've chosen to layer a UDL approach on the Keys to Quality Classroom Assessment from Chappuis, Stiggins, and Arter (2011) as a frame to connect UDL and assessment.

Table 3.4. Classroom assessment and UDL

Key to Classroom Assessment	Description	Questions to assess current state for issues and opportunities	UDL Perspectives
Clear purpose	The assessment is designed to serve the specific information needs of the users. Is it formative? Summative? For licensing? Admissions decisions?	▲ What is the purpose of this assessment? Might be things like formative, summative, placement decisions, external licensing, or admissions. ▲ Who is responsible for the design of this assessment? ▲ Who sees the results? ▲ Why is this assessment needed?	▲ External licensing exams, such as for nursing, are often viewed as a barrier to implementing UDL-informed assessments. Know why certain assessments are used and who makes decisions before making recommendations that can't be implemented. ▲ It may be pragmatic to make changes to the representation of the test than the content. Or teach test-taking strategies to help prepare students for the big test.
Clear targets	The targets for the assessment are clearly articulated and appropriate	▲ What are the goals for this assessment? ▲ How do you know learners have achieved those goals? ▲ What feedback do learners give about this assessment? ▲ Does the assessment align with the learning goal? How could it better align? ▲ How do the goals target both process and product?	▲ Clear goals are totally in the UDL wheelhouse! Expect to spend a lot of time helping instructors unpack the true goal for an assessment. This is time well spent! Don't rush this step.

Key to Classroom Assessment	Description	Questions to assess current state for issues and opportunities	UDL Perspectives
Sound design	The assessment accurately measures what it intends to measure	▲ What does this assessment measure? ▲ What does success look like? ▲ What options are available or could be available for students?	▲ Clear goals, flexible means. Construct-relevance. Be ready to unpack these concepts in plain language. Watch out for tests, presentations, group work, and other formats where the format is often conflated as part of the hidden curriculum but isn't an explicit learning goal.
Effective communication	The results of the assessment are effectively communicated to users	▲ How are the results of this assessment communicated to students? ▲ How many students are in this class? ▲ How are the results used to inform instruction? ▲ What opportunities for feedback or dialogue do students have after the assessment? ▲ What opportunities do you provide for students to have for ongoing feedback during the assessment? ▲ Is feedback specific and meaningful?	▲ Actively informing learners throughout and after the assessment is important to layer a UDL approach. ▲ Be realistic about the situational factors that the instructor is operating under. A class of 200 will provide different opportunities for communication than a class of 25.

Key to Classroom Assessment	Description	Questions to assess current state for issues and opportunities	UDL Perspectives
Student Involvement	Students are involved in self-assessment, goal-setting, tracking, and reflecting on and sharing their learning	▲ How are students involved in the assessment? ▲ How do students track their progress or set goals during the assessment process? ▲ How do students reflect on and share their learning during and after the assessment? ▲ What is the student feedback about this assessment? Do they get excited to tackle it?	▲ Good idea! Some instructors invite students to create questions for test-based assessments or have students co-create study guides or project guides for assignments.

SMART TIP

We often get asked how to "UDL" a test or assessment. Well, here's how we respond to that question! Something isn't UDL or not UDL—it's *how UDL*? Just like as learners and teachers, we are all on a continuum of becoming more expert, we believe that curriculum is on a continuum of being more UDL. We use Meyer, Rose, and Gordon's five elements of effective assessments from a UDL perspective (2014) as our benchmarks. They indicate assessments:

1. Are ongoing and focused on learner progress

2. Measure both product and process

3. Are flexible, not fixed

4. Are construct relevant

5. Actively inform and involve learners

So, for example, we'd ask instructors:

- How are the assessments ongoing and focused on learner progress?

- How can they be more so?

- How do assessments measure both product and process?

- How can they be more so?

We'd also use these items to identify great work already happening. For example, "That rubric you made and shared with students really helped inform them. That's a great practice for UDL." Think of ways that you can try this in your UDL conversations!

A CLOSER LOOK Group work: need we say more? This is a challenging area to assess and is often used as an organizational method rather than being aligned with a learning goal. If the assessment is trying to measure analysis of local environmental factors affecting stream health, but students must work in groups to complete the assessment, is that assessment really measuring what it intends to measure, i.e., the analysis? If group work is critical, encourage instructors to make it part of a clear learning goal and teach and assess the skills and behaviors needed for effective group work. Learn more at http://udloncampus.cast.org/page /assessment

Chose or Create Flexible Methods and Materials to Use in the Instruction. Methods and Materials Need to Align with the Clear Learning Goals and Assessments.

Methods and materials make design come to life and are a significant part of the instructional experience. They are opportunities for creating highly engaging environments, but can also be a stage where simple opportunities are missed that could create significant barriers to accessibility and learning. Layering in a UDL approach to the selection of methods and materials can be highly effective. From a backward design perspective, developing instructional methods and materials enables students to access and engage in learning to achieve the goal. The Guidelines remind us that instruction will be optimized if students can make choices through this process. Draw from the principles, Guidelines, and checkpoints to intentionally and proactively head off barriers (known or anticipated). Consider things in the instructional environment that are going well, or not going well, and work to understand the problem first, and then consider solutions through design.

SKINNY SKETCH
Learning Is Emotional

When I (Eric) looked over the plan of study for my PhD coursework, I was dismayed to see not one, not two, but three mandatory statistics courses, including one my very first term. Having been an English education major and humanities teacher my entire career, I had been avoiding math and math-related fields since 11th grade.

It didn't help that the first stats course was a large class, with the full cohort of PhD students across the entire college of Education, Health, and Human Sciences. My apprehension and aversion to statistics was going to make the course and subsequent learning difficult. I knew it, but knew it the way one knows a sneeze is coming: with a sense of powerlessness to stop it.

With that context, it's hard to overstate how important the first class session was for me. I left the first class feeling excited to learn statistics. How did the instructor change my perspective so effectively?

The first class, rather than using the time to go over the syllabus (which, honestly, would have been overwhelming to me), the instructor handed out a short article about John Snow, whose use of visual data analysis was essential in ending the cholera epidemic in London during the 1850s.

(continued)

Giving us a few minutes to read the article, which set the context, the instructor provided us with a map of the area of London most affected (the same map Snow himself used) and a data set Snow compiled regarding the location of pumps and number of deaths by cholera. We worked together in small groups to map the data in our own ways, and used this data to come to conclusions, which we then had the opportunity to briefly defend to the class (first one group, then any group that disagreed with the conclusion, and so on). Finally, the instructor revealed Snow's marked up map, his conclusions, and the real-world outcome of his work.

We ended with three conclusions:

1. We could "do" statistics. Indeed, we just did.

2. Statistics can be a powerful tool to make sense of data and develop conclusions.

3. Statistics isn't foolproof; there are often multiple interpretations with the same data set.

I was hooked. As the real work of statistics came, this first impression was instrumental in keeping me focused and willing to persist.

Timely Progress Monitoring and Iterative Improvements.

Being an expert teacher means being perpetually willing to learn, make iterative changes, share discoveries, and repeat. This is a great opportunity to share reflective practice cycles with instructors and show them how they can work here, too.

A CLOSER LOOK   For an excellent guide to reflective practice, check out https://bit.ly/2OnxU3U.

Pulling It Together

Helping instructors with teaching is a delicate and important task. Layering a UDL approach and helping instructors learn more about UDL throughout the process is critical work for Navigators and their teams. When working with instructors, focus on helping *them* achieve their stated goal. At the same time, find ways to meaningfully design lessons and experiences that create engaged, expert learners. Use successes to facilitate more opportunities. How can you use that teaching experience to connect with other instructors? How can you build impact, sustainability, and capacity? How could that instructor show their teaching and learning approaches to another instructor?

Because the instructional experience is an intersection of content (curriculum), people (instructors and students), and space (physical or digital), all three aspects must be considered to prepare for successful UDL integration. As a UDL Navigator, your primary focus should be on people. Look for opportunities to support instructors or departments facing challenges for which UDL may help frame solutions. Keep the focus on things over which you and those with whom you collaborate can control or influence. Cultivate relationships with students and instructors so that when barriers come up, you're likely to be brought in to find solutions. Along the way, acknowledge systemic limitations (physical or digital space constraints, administrative barriers, time barriers). Barriers to implementation of UDL plans are just as important to recognize and proactively address when developing implementation strategy as barriers to learning are when designing curriculum and lessons.

 PAUSE AND THINK

- Which teaching and learning environments on your campus have the most systemic barriers to flexible teaching and learning experiences?

- Which of the strategies listed in this chapter do you want to use to try to address these? What strategies would you add?

- What is the most challenging UDL and teaching and learning moment you've had? How did you navigate it?

Whatever methods we use to enhance the learning environment and support students, we should never lose touch with the value of reflection and modification as an ongoing practice. As with any kind of design, an educational design is only as strong as its implementation in practice. Carry out the plan, recognizing opportunities to make adaptations as necessary on the fly. Enable students to offer feedback openly and uncritically so that they can help determine what they need and how the learning experience can be improved yet further in the short term and for "next time." In reflection, carry the mindset that being an expert instructor does not mean getting it "right" (and certainly not the first time!). It is about being willing and able to grow and improve and make changes perpetually to maximize success for everyone.

As you know, teaching and learning is complex work; the strategies provided in this chapter are by no means intended to be exhaustive. But we hope that providing them to you will help you frame your conversations, partnerships, and strategies about integrating UDL and teaching and learning. When clear goals are paired with flexible means of engagement, representation, and action & expression, the nature of learning experiences begins to change and the nature of learning itself changes, too.

Key Takeaways

- Teaching and learning is complex, emotional work. Start UDL conversations by recognizing the effort and care instructors put into their lessons.

- One size does not fit all—choose your approach to supporting instructors with teaching and learning based on the instructors' goals and context.

- UDL is strengths-based! Build on the strengths of the instructor, course, or program and recognize the importance of iterative improvements.

- Position strategies within the UDL framework. The why of strategies is important!

- Connect, don't compete. UDL doesn't have to replace their current approach; just enhance it. "How UDL is it?" not "Is it UDL?".

4

UDL and Technology

Technology is essential for making curricula flexible and accessible. This is because technology has the potential to empower students to adapt and experience material in custom ways (changing size, contrast, clicking extension hyperlinks, etc.) and may remove important accessibility barriers, including print-based barriers. For example, whereas students in a low-tech environment are more reliant on an instructor to explicitly facilitate the options for students (e.g., in how teaching materials are distributed or how teaching occurs), students in accessible high-tech learning environments may choose whether or not to access class material on their own devices, opt to turn captioning on or off, adjust contrast or the size of text, opt to use text-to-speech software to read their text-based material, and so forth.

Why It Matters

The fact that UDL has a strong relationship with technology is important in part because this provides an opportunity to develop UDL as a "joint initiative" with the existing push for higher levels of technology in the classroom (or classrooms hosted online!). In fact, applying UDL principles may be a critical way to frame positive use of technology in the classroom and head off known barriers associated with technology (e.g., learner distraction). That said, technology deployment and UDL should always be viewed as complementary, not codependent. Instructors in lower-tech or no-tech environments may still use the UDL design principles and Guidelines to intentionally reach more students and enhance the learning experience. However, such application is necessarily more teacher-dependent and thus is both more time-intensive for instructors and option-poor for learners.

Technology allows skilled learners to make independent choices to render the learning experience more tailored to their needs, preferences, and skills. Therefore, with more technology-rich environments the *potential* to realize learner expertise and provide learner options is greater.

Getting Our Bearings

While there are many forms of technology, including discipline-specific tools, which may be used as part of UDL design to enhance learning, in this chapter we want to focus more specifically on personal mobile devices, including laptops, tablets, and smartphones. We now have more smartphones in the world than human beings (Boren, 2014). Mobile devices and technologies have significant influence in our lives, including how we socialize, work, and play. They may also transform how we learn— if they're allowed to. Students in higher education may know how to use their phones and laptops to do many incredible things, but struggle to use them to take notes, organize resources, or perform other tasks that would enhance their learning and develop their skills that could transfer to the workforce. This has created a vicious cycle whereby many instructors feel (often rightly) that digital devices are a distraction to students and thus should not be used in class. As a result, students are not always taught how to use their devices as powerful tools of learning, so when they are casually allowed to keep their laptops open in class, they may well fall into distraction and the cycle continues.

There is copious and contradictory evidence about the value of mobile devices in the classroom. We like to call this "The Great Mobile Device Debate." Many researchers suggest that digital devices have a negative effect on student engagement and performance and also that of their peers (e.g., Bowman, Levine, Waite, Gendron, 2010; Fried, 2008; Sana, Weston, & Cepeda, 2013; Sana, Weston, & Cepeda, 2013; Tossell, Kortum, Shepard, Rahmati, & Zhong, 2015). Many others say the exact opposite (Barry, Murphy, & Drew, 2015; Gulek & Demirtas, 2005; Conole, de Laat, Dillon, & Darby, 2008; Junco, 2012; Kay & Lauricella, 2011; Roberts & Rees, 2014). These publications, among others, explore topics like note taking, student engagement, and academic achievement and repeatedly come to opposing conclusions. Even as postsecondary institutions try to increase technology use on campus, they may get significant pushback from instructors who consider the addition of fancy technology and mobile devices as detrimental to the community and quality of learning in class.

So, which is it? Is technology good or bad in the hands of higher education students? This is the wrong question. What is becoming clear is that the success or failure of technology in the classroom has much more to do with how it is used and the intentionality of its use than whether or not it is used. Students need to learn how to use technology as a tool that, like any other tool, is powerful if applied well and in the right context, and deleterious if used poorly or in the wrong context.

What does this have to do with UDL? Remember from Chapter 2, "UDL and Course-Level Design," and Chapter 3, "UDL + Teaching and Learning," that curriculum and learning experiences are only as effective as they are *designed* to be. Just as no instructional practice is a silver bullet that will work in all contexts for all purposes, so no technology or device is going to be relevant, useful, or helpful in all situations. By using UDL to design the learning experience from goals through assessment, methods, and materials, we can be cognizant about when, where, why, and for what function technology may be useful (and also know when it's not!). This enables us to support administrators, instructors, and students in making decisions that put the right tools in students' hands at the right times.

Taking Action: Facilitating Buy-in

The "Great Mobile Device Debate" is an important opportunity for facilitating administrator and instructor buy-in. Remember, being a UDL Navigator involves addressing real, predictable barriers to improve the quality of teaching and learning. Consider the following conversation between an instructor and a UDL Navigator:

> **Instructor:** I'm getting a lot of negative feedback from students about my policy banning laptops and

smartphones in my classroom. I hate feeling like I am having to restrict my adult students in this way, but honestly, I just got burned out by how distracted they became by texting and Facebook and who knows what. And when the articles started to come out about how the worse effect may be "collateral" disengagement from non-device-using peers who are distracted by those who do use them, I decided it was a moral obligation to take a stand.

UDL Navigator: That's an important barrier you're addressing. Student engagement is critical, and like you said, there is a lot of research regarding the correlation of laptops and student distraction in the classroom. But I also hear that in addressing one barrier, another one is coming up in students feeling upset about not being able to use their devices, right?

Instructor: Right.

Note how this conversation began. The UDL Navigator is listening and making sure he or she understands the barrier as the instructor experiences it. This is the first step. Now watch as the UDL Navigator seeks to facilitate the "paradigm shift" from "student issue" to "environmental issue."

UDL Navigator: So, what I am hearing is that there's a "conflict of access" here, where the presence of laptops seems to hinder in some ways, and their absence hinders in other ways. What would be ideal is if we could find a way to address both of these opposing barriers.

Instructor: I can see that. That makes some sense.

UDL Navigator: Great! You know, there's a common assumption that today's college students excel with technical knowledge. And in some ways that may be true, but just because students know how to use their computers well for communicating, finding information, gaming, and so on, that doesn't mean that they know how to use them for learning or how to manage their use. To me, this is an opportunity to teach them "soft skills" related to technology such as management and how to use them for learning, while addressing the need for maintaining engagement in class.

Did you notice how the attention subtly shifted from student-problem to environment (lack of intentionality, lack of opportunity for growth)? This shift needs to be done in such a way that it empowers instructors rather than pinning blame on them. That's what the UDL Navigator strove for in this case. The instructor is now engaged and wanting to learn more about strategies to address the environmental problem. Now, we're ready to draw from UDL principles and checkpoints to explore clear goals and ways that technology can be used effectively.

In this case, the instructor came in with a ready-made barrier, which made it easy to accomplish the first step of identifying a barrier and enabled us to focus our energies on shifting the perspective of the barrier and then addressing it through UDL.

But what if someone is coming to the UDL Navigator with the promise of technology and no recognition of the barriers that technology may introduce? Check out the following scenario to see how a UDL Navigator could handle this.

Instructor: I'm so excited to share! My department just won a grant to purchase a full class set of iPads for our lecture halls, which can be used with our new high-tech podium that will allow for students to respond to questions, share their screens, etcetera. I'm really hopeful that these will help students learn and engage with the material!

UDL Navigator: That's wonderful! I am so excited for you and your students! You're right on that having access to technology can really be a great asset in the lecture hall! How can I help you with this?

Nice move, UDL Navigator. We don't want to force the barrier on the instructor. Their enthusiasm is a great thing and an important asset. If they are talking to the UDL specialist, they may have some sense of reservation or they may know that they don't know what barriers may lie ahead (which is itself a barrier). The point is to allow them to give initial direction. Nothing is worse than listening to someone explain how to solve a problem you don't think you have.

Instructor: Well, here's the thing. I'm in charge of getting the iPads all set up. There are so many options and I don't know where to begin choosing the right apps and whatnot for the iPads. I guess I am looking for some ideas as to what's good! What's out there?

UDL Navigator: That's a great question! I have lots of recommendations, but they depend a lot on what you want your students to do with the iPads. What's your learning goal in this lesson? You mentioned student response during lectures; can you tell me more about that? What was hard about student response without iPads?

This is a variation of the problem we saw in the first scenario. The instructor feels like the technology itself will make things better and wants to maximize the quality of the technology. The UDL specialist is going to want to address the question directly and completely, but also shift the perspective to help the instructor think beyond the devices to the environment.

After some back-and-forth like this, the UDL Navigator will have a clear sense of the barriers and opportunities that the instructor is attempting to address with the iPads. Without being negative at all, the UDL Navigator has opened the opportunity to discuss when and why the use of iPads will be effective (according to UDL principles and checkpoints) and is able to effectively and efficiently guide the instructor in some recommended applications to install on the iPads.

Later, if time permits, after the instructor's immediate question and needs have been met, the UDL Navigator may also wish to introduce the instructor to some potential barriers related to device misuse and discuss how the strategies they've already brainstormed can help proactively prevent these; the UDL Navigator may also discuss ideas for how to address issues that do arise despite proactive measures. The key here was to shift thinking away from seeing students or technology as the barrier or solution and moving the barrier (and solution) to where it belongs: on the environment.

Winning over Administrators

Accessibility is a hot topic in higher education. In a time when postsecondary institutions are being sued for accessibility issues and awareness of needs for accessible design are both peaking, UDL Navigators have more opportunity than ever to support proactive accessible design such as that afforded by UDL and made efficient by technology.

There's also growing recognition that accessibility must extend beyond simply meeting the needs of students with disabilities. Many higher-education institutions have been struggling to retain and graduate students who are diverse in other ways, including those who are first-generation college students, or from low-income families. Improving accessibility is a way to help prevent lawsuits and improve retention and graduation rates: all things that administrators tend to value highly.

Again, we believe that the success of UDL implementation is strongly related to the degree to which we can successfully create "joint initiatives" whereby UDL is used to enhance an existing initiative or pain point. The strong relationship among accessibility, technology, and UDL makes for a great opportunity to cultivate administrative buy-in. The nice thing about this is that it doesn't matter which of the three initiatives administration chooses to push first—whichever it is, the other two can quickly be associated.

For example, consider how common technology can be used to facilitate both accessibility and UDL. Read&Write (by Texthelp) is a literacy software and screen reader for sighted people who benefit from audio-based support when reading. A site license for Read&Write or similar software provides access to technology that, if used, may equip students with dyslexia or other reading or visual challenges to access reading materials, including text documents, PDFs, PowerPoints, or HTML content such as in learning management systems. But the benefits also extend to students without disabilities. They may benefit being able to listen and read simultaneously, which some students find to be highly effective to support their learning (Rao, Ok, & Bryant, 2014). The speech-to-text features also support students in writing first drafts or note taking. Hearing one's own writing read aloud via the text-to-speech feature can facilitate revision. When students are coached in how to use the software, as well as what their options are, they can make better decisions regarding how to learn in different circumstances. In this example, we are able to demonstrate that wonderful claim that UDL so often speaks to, that "what is essential for some is good for all" (Meyer, Rose, & Gordon, 2014, p. 86).

Goals First; Technology Second

Recall our discussions in Chapters 2 and Chapter 3 about how UDL can inform the learning design process. In learning design, everything is based on supporting learners toward the intended outcome(s). This means that we should encourage instructors and administrators to avoid starting with "we want students to use [insert technology]." This puts the methods ahead of the objective, which is counterproductive in UDL. Rather, instructors and administrators should consider technology that is appropriate and useful for supporting diverse students as they strive toward the learning outcomes by providing for a greater range of engagement, representation, or self-expression than could be had without the technology tool.

PAUSE AND THINK

- How might your or others' views of technology influence how it is used (or not) in the classroom?

- How might well-intended overt bans on mobile technology negatively affect some students more than others (e.g., those with disclosed or undisclosed disabilities, English language learners)?

- How might using UDL in teaching and learning influence how, when, and why instructors call for students to use technology intentionally?

- How would you help instructors balance supporting executive functioning and attention in the classroom with the use of personal mobile devices?

For example, a composition instructor may have an outcome related to students being able to compose rhetorical arguments in speech and short essay format. That instructor may realize proactively that many students find rhetoric easier in spoken form than written (or vice versa). Without changing or reducing the outcome, the instructor may think about how to train students to use speech-to-text software to convert spoken rhetorical arguments into print, and how to then edit the resulting text for clarity and formatting.

This approach would call for technology (tablets or laptops equipped with speech-to-text software) and a little coaching. The result? More students would feel successful with the final product *and* would know how to use this tool to express themselves in other contexts (e.g., other classes, writing reports for future jobs). Students for whom typing was difficult (due to a physical or learning disability) may not need additional accommodations and so could learn and interact on pace with others in the class using the same technology.

Pulling It Together

In this chapter, we explored some of the ways that the use of personal mobile devices by students is already occurring in higher education and how this provides opportunity for a "joint initiative" with UDL. Technology is only as good as its usage. UDL offers a powerful framework for using technology effectively, and thus may be used to facilitate buy-in from both instructors and administrators. Just as UDL can be applied without technology, so can technology be used without regard for the UDL principles, but what is abundantly clear from our experience is that they are better together.

Key Takeaways

- Goals first; technology second. The success or failure of technology in the classroom has much more to do with how it is used and the intentionality of its use than whether or not it is used.

- Essential for some; good for all. Strategic use of personal mobile technology can proactively remove accessibility barriers for some learners and support personalization for all.

- Consider making purposeful technology use its own learning goal. Learners may need coaching on how to use technology to support their own learning, but it will be worth it. Managing distractions and technologies is a skill students (and we!) need in class and the workforce.

5

UDL and Accessibility Services

While known by different names, such as *student disability services*, the *office of disability support*, or the *accessibility services (AS) office* (which is the term we will use in this chapter) is a key resource and partner for a UDL Navigator. While many student services offices are important partners for a UDL Navigator, because of the history of UDL being connected with disability, there is an important impact of partnering and having a cohesive understanding of accessibility and UDL. UDL is focused on engaging student learning experiences, and the stakeholders in that goal go beyond the classroom.

Why It Matters

The Accessibility Services staff are established campus experts in disability and providing services and supports for students with disabilities in higher education. In some offices, they also have teaching and design expertise and are available to partner with instructors to improve the accessibility of their academic environment. The AS staff have expertise that is critical to helping others learn about learning variability, disability, and design. How they present students with disabilities and the nature of disability itself is a major factor in how disability is perceived on campus. They can make or break the linguistic, conceptual, attitudinal foundation on which a UDL culture is to be built. Enlisting their partnership in presenting disability as a difference, not a deficit, and working from a social, not medical, model of disability will be critical to furthering your UDL work.

AS offices are also the gateway to academic accommodations, which makes the services they provide a critical part of the student experience for many learners, and teaching experience for many instructors. They have multiple interactions with students who may experience environmental or learning barriers, which positions them to shift the conversation from disability to variability and from response to design. AS staff can also use their role with instructors to plant seeds of interest in UDL and build the UDL community on campus through referrals to UDL specialists, or may even pioneer a UDL community. The interaction of academic accommodations and UDL is important practically and strategically as an opportunity for change management.

 A CLOSER LOOK   For more on the integration of inclusive learning practices and disability accomodations, check out this wonderful position paper on inclusive education in higher education from the Association for Higher Education Access and Disability (AHEAD) in Ireland: https://bit.ly/2THTsed.

A NOTE ON LANGUAGE:
Identity First vs. People First

Language matters, and people often have strong feelings and response to language surrounding human disability. Some people in the disability community prefer what is known as *identity first language*. That is: they prefer to be called *autistic people* or *deaf people*, or *disabled students,* for example. This is often the preference of disabled people. On the other hand, there are also proponents of *people first language* who prefer *people with autism* or *people who are deaf* or *students with disabilities* for example. Some people with disabilities prefer this language.

There are reasons and rationales for both of these perspectives that are beyond the scope of this work. We chose to use people first language in this work because it is more commonly used in higher education conversations, often required by journal publishers, and corresponds with the current UN definition of disability and other major policies in several nations. However, we both respect and value the discussion around this topic and strongly advocate respecting the wishes of individuals.

In your work, talk with your team members and disability community members about what language you will use. Also, consider how to address outdated language and use it as a learning opportunity without shutting down dialogue.

Getting Our Bearings

Because UDL has roots in universal design (UD) and emphasizes proactively removing barriers for everyone (including individuals with disabilities), the UDL Navigator will find a trusted and established ally in Accessibility Services. Indeed, AS staff are ready-made champions for the increased accessibility and barrier removal that UDL aims to bring about. UDL Navigators may find a willing partner in AS to cooperatively facilitate institutional change with UDL initiatives. Such a partnership is win-win for everyone.

Keep in mind that AS offices often operate under budgetary, legislative, historical, and attitudinal constraints that may limit them, for better or for worse, to service provision. Additionally, AS staff often have heavy workloads as they seek to make the best decisions possible to support their learners and instructors. In partnership, AS and UDL Navigators can proactively work to reduce barriers and increase accessibility for everyone. Doing so thereby reduces the accommodations needed by students with disabilities while enhancing the learning experience for everyone.

It also bears noting that AS and UDL Navigators may have different emphases and therefore different perspectives on the key concepts of UDL. Taking the time to align language and understanding is critical to ensuring an accurate and consistent message about UDL to campus stakeholders. An example is the word *accessibility*. Some may view accessibility in terms of physical spaces and access to content for individuals with disabilities, while others may want to expand the meaning of accessibility to a broader access to learning and expert learning for everyone. You may extend this example to comparing the terms *accommodation*, *accessibility,* and *UDL* because sometimes those are inaccurately used interchangeably.

Another potential challenge this office faces is the misperception of UDL as solely a disability or accessibility initiative. UDL began in the context of special education but has since grown to achieve a true universal intent. Because of this, there is a danger in over-associating UDL and accommodations, facilitated by residual association of UDL with exclusively supporting students with disabilities. Sometimes there is confusion between concepts that share roots in improving access for students with disabilities, including differentiation, academic accommodations, universal design (UD), Universal Instructional Design (UID), and UDL. As a UDL Navigator, you need to be explicit about your language and do not assume that everyone shares the same vocabulary. There are many different stages of integration, awareness, readiness, and change within disability services departments. Don't assume that everyone is using key terms in the same way. Taking the time to double check language and meanings is a critical component for working successfully with AS departments.

 A CLOSER LOOK See Eric's blog post "Isn't UDL Just...?" to see how we parse UDL from some commonly confused constructs (including differentiated instruction, accommodations, and WCAG 2.0). Go to http://innospire.org /isnt-udl-just/.

Taking Action: Strategic Partnerships

As UDL Navigators collaborating with AS, we need to be attuned to and respectful of their specific mission; we need to look for opportunities to support their mission, and forge relationships that foster collaboration. There are many opportunities for overlap, and these strategic partnerships are key for a UDL Navigator! In Eric's context, for example, a strong collegial relationship with the AS team has led to bilateral instructor referrals, joint workshops and trainings, and even the opportunity to be on the search committee for an AS assistant director position. All of this has enabled the shared values of creating a more accessible and effective learning experience for everyone, to be realized through ongoing joint efforts.

Capitalize on opportunities.   At every campus there will be unique opportunities. They will be contextual, so keep your eye out! Mine these interactions and see opportunities where others see problems. Often the opportunities come from pain points. AS staff are well-attuned to known trouble spots on campus for students with disabilities. For example, if students are struggling significantly due to a lack of captioned media, which puts burden on AS, that knowledge enables the UDL Navigator to campaign for a campus-wide captioning initiative through training and/or a systematic process for captioning media for the benefit of *all* learners, not just those registered with the AS office.

PAUSE AND THINK

▢ UDL is commonly (and incorrectly) understood to be a framework that is explicitly *for students with disabilities.* How would you respond to a colleague who expressed this misunderstanding?

▢ What are the strengths and limitations of the AS office in your context? How can you connect with them to harness their strengths and support their limitations to facilitate a mutually beneficial relationship?

▢ What pain points does the AS team at your institution have? How could a UDL approach help solve some of those problems?

Other pain points that the AS staff may recognize include everyday things like instructors needing to use new technology for an accommodation, questions about the "fairness" of some students using assistive technologies, or larger issues such as human rights issues or lawsuits. Each of these may invite opportunities for learning, training, or facilitating administrative support to connect a disability-specific situation to a UDL solution.

Build relationships. Building relationships is the cornerstone of UDL change. Position yourself as a fellow learner; model the UDL approach. Everyone has expertise if they are growing, and we know that no one is ever done growing or learning. Find champions in the AS office and see what opportunities there could be to partner. Whether it's designing a professional development opportunity, sharing referral sources, or just learning more about each other's processes, this is a key relationship. It's important for all to know that a UDL initiative doesn't mean that accommodations will automatically stop. We suggest using a visual to help teams understand that accommodation planning and provision does not stop as soon as a UDL initiative starts.

Build on strengths. Identify what's already happening to support inclusive learning and instructor development and build on it. Maybe your AS team has outstanding instructor relationships, proactively supports student development, or has an innovative UDL project on the go! Systemic growth opportunities could come through partnering with a team that is already making changes or redesigning policies, processes, and procedures—your work would add value to those changes that are already underway. As we say: connect, don't compete.

Create professional learning opportunities. Professionals who have a passion for systemic change and making improvements to school environments will enhance the experience of students with disabilities.

Facilitating and creating partnerships to provide professional learning opportunities for instructors can be an excellent interdepartmental opportunity for you to facilitate UDL-based change. Bringing multiple perspectives to UDL professional learning opportunities can be an excellent way to enhance meaning and authenticity. Often, the AS team knows engaged students who are happy to share their experiences in the learning environment.

Clarify the interactions between accommodations, accessibility, and UDL.   Clarifying the interactions between accommodations, accessibility, and UDL may help clarify how each area works together. For the uninitiated, these terms may seem interchangeable, but they are importantly distinct. Clarifying the overlaps may create more space for collaborative opportunities! Please add your own examples and terms to make the chart make more sense in the context of your institution.

Facilitate changes to process and policy.   When processes are up for review or policies are up for renewal, this can be an outstanding opportunity to partner with AS to integrate some UDL bridges. Accommodation planning processes could lead to referrals for instructors to have proactive UDL support. Closed captioning initiatives could combine with instructors' professional learning about how to add closed captions. Assistive technology purchases could align with budgeting time for departments to buy equipment that would help all students. For example, one student needed a visual stethoscope and all the other students wanted to use it too. The instructor saw this and made sure she ordered some as classroom learning tools. What's essential for one can be good for all!

 SKINNY SKETCH
Accessing Access

Eric recently met with a doctoral student in communications whose dissertation would be a qualitative analysis of the lived experience of students with disabilities in the college context. In conversation with him about UDL, he was thrilled with the vision. He suggested that students with disabilities often have to expend significant emotional, physical, or practical effort and time obtaining supports just to arrive at step one where many of their peers began.

This may mean reduced capacity to engage or keep up with their peers and add to a sense of burden on the student, the instructor, and the school at large. UDL helps address this by proactively providing for diverse students (including those with disabilities), in some cases removing the necessity of specialized accommodations and in all cases reducing the number of steps some students need to take to get to step 1 in their learning process. Thus, UDL may work to simultaneously enhance and reduce the necessity of special accommodation for students, while greatly improving their lived experience and ease of learning in higher education.

Pulling It Together

Accessibility services staff are institutional leaders promoting inclusivity and facilitating the accommodation processes and more for students with disabilities. They are key partners for you as a UDL Navigator. They are often powerful allies when everyone is able to see how UDL and accessibility intersect and are synergistic. AS staff can help amplify the message of UDL, functioning as key connectors of instructors to UDL Navigators, by promoting shared language (differentiating among UDL, accessibility, and accommodations), and by identifying opportunities and trouble spots that may be well served by a UDL approach.

 SMART TIP   As Black and Fraser (2019) note, AS can play an important leadership role in shifting faculty mindsets. Here are five important shifts: 1) medical to social model of disability, 2) learning labels to learning variability, 3) response to design, 4) accessibility to expert learning, and 5) ad hoc to intentionality.

Key Takeaways

▫ The accessibility services office and its staff are powerful allies in the mission of inclusion and UDL integration.

▫ It is valuable to build common language and conceptualization regarding disability, inclusion, accessibility, and Universal Design for Learning.

▫ It's helpful to partner with AS staff to collaborate on joint initiatives toward more complete models of inclusion.

▫ They are often attuned to pain points regarding learner inclusion and the experience of students with disabilities.

6

UDL and
Professional Learning

When we talk about UDL, we usually focus on the students as our primary motivation and beneficiaries—sensibly so! While developing expert learners is, indeed, a primary goal of our work as UDL practitioners, we must take a larger view in our role as UDL Navigators. After all, we are change agents for the system as a whole, and that includes developed expert learners, teachers, and systems.

Why It Matters

From a systems perspective, expert learners are cultivated by expert teachers who develop as part of expert systems. In our context, we define an expert teacher or instructor as one who cultivates his or her own development, embraces change, and continuously appraises their own work and their students' progress (Meyer, Rose & Gordon, 2014). While individual instructors may practice UDL in their classrooms, UDL becomes increasingly effective as it is integrated into whole departments, programs, colleges, and universities. Therefore, UDL is most successful in the context of expert systems; that is, institutions that are intentionally designed to provide ongoing learning experiences that encourage, enable, and equip expert instructors who are invested in the development of expert learners. In this way, professional learning joins with community building at the heart of expert systems.

Getting Our Bearings

As UDL Navigators, we must be intentional about promoting a UDL approach to professional learning. When we say, "A UDL approach to professional learning," we don't just mean creating and cultivating experiences where instructors learn about UDL. We mean infusing and modeling a UDL approach to *all* professional learning opportunities as we model UDL and support instructors as professional learners who continue to pursue excellence in teaching as well as their subject matter. Because UDL is both our frame for the design and delivery of learning experiences and also the content about which we may sometimes teach, we should model UDL practices even when explicitly teaching about UDL.

Regardless of the content being addressed during professional learning opportunities (e.g., mobile device use, diversity and inclusion, accessibility, lesson design, technology training) we should keep in mind a few key ideas.

Instructors as learners In the context of professional learning, instructors, like any other learners, are highly and predictably variable in how they learn and engage with the material. Professional learning experiences must predict and design for that variability in the same ways that we expect those same instructors to design for their variable students. Keep in mind, not all instructors are comfortable with being in the learner's seat. They are used to being experts in their field, and they may be more comfortable as a subject matter expert than as a professional learner. That's just another reason that modeling UDL in a professional learning experience can be a meaningful way to remind instructor-learners about how highly variable human learning is.

As with all learners, instructors in professional development experiences need learning to be challenging, not threatening. So, when we teach instructors about UDL, for example, it's important to use strategies to demystify the topic, build on instructors' own strengths and examples, emphasizing growth over perfection, and connect it to their own teaching and learning goals. All of these can help make UDL feel more relevant and less threatening to instructors.

"Training" or "learning" orientation? Considering how you, your colleagues, and your school view professional learning experiences may offer insight into your strategy for integrating a UDL approach into professional learning. To us, training is often a transactional model—a transfer of knowledge or skills that is compliance- or competency-based. We need "training" on student rights, using learning management systems, or first aid. The goals are often externally determined, and everyone is on the same learning path at the same time.

When we talk about professional learning experiences, we mean experiences that are highly individual and learning-centered, and more than just the transmission of content. Such experiences are the product of design, intended to create the highest quality and variety of experiences for our instructor-learners to reach their professional learning goals. While individuals may share an experience (like a course or a session), their own professional learning will differ depending on many things, including their learning goals, strengths, needs, and context.

Dual professionals   Few instructors outside of schools of education come with formal education in teaching and learning. Instructors arrive with deep expertise in their trade, profession, or field of study. This is critical to what they bring to the learning experience in higher education. For students, learning from experts is an amazing opportunity. However, these instructors may not yet know or be highly skilled in the art and science of supporting others in learning what they know. Indeed, when industry experts become educators, they may undergo an identity transformation. No longer are they only nurses, geologists, or accountants, they are also educators. As educators, they will need to learn the tools of this teaching and learning trade to develop their professional identity and expertise as educators in higher education. In this sense, they are becoming dual professionals.

Instructors' professional learning journeys and choices will also have to balance this dual professional identity. Instructors need to maintain currency, connection, research in their fields, trades, or professions, as well as develop their teaching and learning skills and mindset. As a UDL Navigator, it's important to keep this in mind when planning and working with professional learning experiences for instructors in higher education. One of the main opportunities we have is to help influence instructors' identities as educators and what that means to them. What do they want students to learn? How do they want to feel when working with their students? What do they hope students remember years after they've left the class? Shifting from content to learning is an important shift that a UDL approach can help foster in instructors who are continuously building their identities as dual professionals.

Professional learning systems   If we want to build professional learning opportunities for instructors, it helps to understand the current state and possibilities that exist within the system that financially supports professional learning. What situational factors support (or inhibit) professional learning at your institution? For example, who makes the decisions about professional learning budgets? How are instructors compensated for their time? Who has leadership roles in professional learning? Human Resources and the Center for Teaching and Learning may have different priorities or approaches to creating, developing, and measuring professional learning. As a UDL Navigator committed to fostering and growing professional learning opportunities that support and model UDL, you'll need to befriend many stakeholders across your institution. Even if UDL isn't on the agenda, you can influence professional learning systems by modeling a learning-centered, not topic-centered, approach, and by creating situations and spaces that your instructor-learners want to be in.

Taking Action: Building Expertise

As with any learning experience, professional learning can follow a design process. Consider what processes will work best for your designs and consider how the instructor-learners can be involved with the design process. Intentionally model a UDL approach, Navigator!

Clear goals   As with any educational endeavor, building professional learning experiences requires clear goals. While there may be learning goals, like improving intentional integration of UDL approaches, we'd suggest that one goal connect to building community. Make it an explicit goal. Ways to build community could look very different, and that's good! It's important that the community owns the process of creating and building your learning community. Within any strategic direction, keep your own principles in play, and we recommend relationship building as being a key principle of professional learning.

Professional learning communities   Professional learning communities (PLCs) can be a powerful way to create lasting change with an educational team. Ongoing, goal-oriented, and collaborative, PLCs provide a co-created professional learning environment for instructors to develop their UDL mindset, skills, and actions. PLCs can take many forms and the individuals within the PLC can decide the direction. Examples may include book studies, course planning, or questions of practice. Having the instructor-learners at the center of the design is key and is an opportunity to model the UDL Guidelines in action in a non-classroom learning environment.

Modeling the framework   In any professional learning situation, you may take action simply by intentionally modeling the UDL framework in the design of the learning experience. Whatever the topic or content of the learning experience, UDL can still be modeled and showcased through the design. This can be a powerful way to introduce UDL to a variety of audiences and model it, without UDL itself being the content focus of the professional learning. In other words, *use* UDL to teach instructors how to utilize a new learning management system (LMS), develop effective assessments, or engage students in the lecture hall.

This can work well when looking to partner with existing professional learning opportunities, like a workshop series. You could offer to review their existing offerings through a UDL lens and offer recommendations for increasing the intentional use of UDL and explaining how that would remove barriers, improve engagement, and support professional learning for all. You could also partner with others on the intentional design of professional learning experiences and help model UDL along the way through the design process. Of course, you can also offer UDL-specific learning experiences that model UDL (of course!) and have UDL content.

Look for other relationship-building opportunities and non-traditional learning spaces to intentionally and transparently infuse a UDL approach. One key area is meetings. Strong meetings include many UDL elements such as clear goals, flexible options, checking for understanding, and multiple representations. Using your UDL navigation skills, you may uncover non-traditional learning spaces to model UDL and keep all people immersed in and exposed to UDL learning experiences.

PAUSE AND THINK

- What is the professional learning culture at your organization? What opportunities and obstacles are there to infusing a UDL approach? What strategies would help you (and your teams) capitalize on the opportunities and overcome the obstacles?

- What are your professional learning principles? What are your institution's? What are UDL's? Look for ways to apply those or advance those in different areas of your institution.

- Do you focus more on UDL content or modeling? What's the best mix for you? What do you think is most appropriate for your instructors? If the focus is content, what level is the right level to start?

- Find the strengths of individuals and teams and work to collaboratively build them. How would you build on the strengths of your teams?

Whenever reasonably possible, it's very important to be explicit when you model UDL. That is, draw attention to the fact that modeling is being employed by showcasing how the learning experience intentionally included UDL design elements. Emphasizing intentionality is key. Try adding a summary page about where you included clear goals and multiple means.

From small choices, like sharing a clear learning goal, to larger choices, like providing student-driven options for assessments, you can showcase how intentionally using the UDL framework informed your planning.

Another strategy, if they are ready, is to have *them* identify what UDL design elements were present in the learning experience! The approach of explicit modeling of UDL has proven a powerful approach to support instructors who are more likely to change their approach to teaching based on positive experiences *with* UDL compared to simply being told *about* UDL.

Infusing and improving existing initiatives and systems   It is also valuable to determine if there are existing initiatives, from policy development to onboarding of new instructors to providing on-demand IT support to new program development. Perhaps there is a grant opportunity. Each policy, process, or initiative is also a learning opportunity that you can seize as a UDL Navigator. As UDL Navigators, we need to think of our schools as living, breathing systems that must learn to grow, change, and improve. That learning can be planned for and modeled using a UDL approach.

Pulling It Together

In higher education, we believe that all environments can be learning environments. With all types of professional learning opportunities, intentionally and transparently applying the UDL Guidelines is at the core of the work as much as learning about UDL. Be the voice at the table that introduces the Guidelines, asks about goals, asks about options, and asks about expertise. Bring these elements to the conversations and help others be ready to bring those questions to planning conversations, as well. Be ready with examples, anecdotes, and testimonials about a UDL approach. Consider your own organization: What problems are they trying to solve or what mountains are they trying to climb? How can UDL be a meaningful contribution to that, not an add-on?

Also, consider yourself and your role as a learner. While you are a proud UDL Navigator, you, like everyone else, are first a learner. We suggest you wear that badge proudly! Model that expertise as a journey of intentional growth, sharing, and improvement, not a static badge.

Key Takeaways

- Build expertise. UDL integration requires a systemic approach that intentionally develops expert learners, teaching, and systems.

- Model, model, model! UDL professional learning doesn't just mean such development that explicitly focuses on UDL; it means using UDL to design and deliver any and all professional development in the higher-education context.

- Instructors are learners, too. Just as we proactively identify and design to address potential barriers for learners, so we need to proactively address barriers that would hinder instructors from learning or practicing UDL.

Epilogue

On any voyage or expedition, the navigator may often be overlooked by casual observers, but the presence of a skilled navigator will usually determine success or failure. Likewise, being a UDL Navigator is a critical, guiding role focused on servant leadership. In our experience, success for UDL in institutions of higher education is founded on relationship-building, collaboration, co-visioning, and a slow nurturing of shared values in inclusion, engagement, and design for variability.

It's worth noting that institutions of higher education have immense inertia that can make the kind of deep cultural change we UDL Navigators advocate for a very slow process. As you do the work of collaborating, supporting, documenting, and recruiting as a UDL Navigator, remember that progress is measured iteratively. Keep the big picture in mind, but measure progress in increments. The work we UDL Navigators are doing has the potential to significantly alter higher education for the better; such change is as slow as it is valuable and radical. Collectively, we must maintain patience and persistence as we stay the course of learning and leading. We must always point ahead of ourselves as well as others. This is the call of a Navigator. Welcome to the team.

References

Barry, S., Murphy, K., & Drew, S. (2015). From deconstructive misalignment to constructive alignment: Exploring student uses of mobile technologies in university classrooms. *Computers & Education, 81*, 202–210.

Berquist, E. (2017). Using the UDL framework as a guide for professional learning. In E. Berquist (Ed.), *UDL: Moving from exploration to integration* (3–18). Wakefield, MA: CAST.

Berquist, E., Carey, L., Ralabate, P.K., & Sadera, W. (2017). Changing beliefs: A view inside a coaching experience based on UDL. In E. Berquist (Ed.), *UDL: Moving from exploration to integration* (19–31), Wakefield, MA: CAST.

Black, J., & Fraser, R. (2019). Integration through collaboration: Building strategic faculty partnerships to shift minds and practices. In S. Braken & K. Novak (Eds.), *Transforming higher education through universal design for learning: An international perspective* (pp. 244-257). London: Routledge.

Boren, Z. (2014). There are officially more smartphones than there are people in the world. *Independent.* Retrieved from https://www.independent.co.uk/life-style/gadgets-and-tech/news/there-are-officially-more-mobile-devices-than-people-in-the-world-9780518.html

Bowman, L., Levine, L, Waite, B, & Gendron, M. (2010). Can students really multitask? An experimental study of instant messaging while reading. *Computers & Education, 54*(4), 927–931.

Center for Applied Special Technology (CAST). (2018). *Universal Design for Learning Guidelines,* version 2.2. Wakefield, MA: National Center on Universal Design for Learning.

Chappuis J., Stiggins R., Arter J., & Chappuis, S. (2011). *Classroom assessment for student learning.* New York, NY: Pearson.

Conole, G., Darby, J., De Laat, M., & Dillon, T. (2008). 'Disruptive technologies', 'pedagogical innovation': What's new? Findings from an in-depth study of students' use and perception of technology. *Computers and Education, 50*(2), 511-524.

Davies, P.L., Schelly, C.L., & Spooner, C.L. (2013). Measuring the effectiveness of universal design for learning intervention in postsecondary education. *Journal of Postsecondary Education and Disability, 26*(3), 195-220.

Eisner, E.W. (2013). What does it mean to say a school is doing well? In D.J. Flinders and S.J. Thornton (Eds.), *The curriculum studies reader* (279–287). New York, NY: Routledge.

Elliott, K., & Healy, M. (2001). Key factors influencing student satisfaction related to recruitment and retention. *Journal of Marketing for Higher Education, 10*(4), 1-11.

Fink, L.D. (2003). *A self-directed guide to designing course for significant learning.* Norman, OK: Dee Fink and Associates. Retrieved from https://bit.ly/2q2Ano3

Fried, C.B. (2008). In-class laptop use and its effects on student learning. *Computers & Education, 50*(3), 906–914. https://doi.org/10.1016/j.compedu.2006.09.006

Gulek, J. C., & Demirtas, H. (2005). Learning with technology: The impact of laptop use on student achievement. *The Journal of Technology, Learning and Assessment, 3*(2). Retrieved from https://ejournals.bc.edu/ojs/index.php/jtla/article/view/1655

Izzo, M.V., Murray, A., & Novak, J. (2008). The faculty perspective on universal design for learning. *Journal of Postsecondary Education and Disability, 21*(2), 60–72.

Junco, R. (2012). In-class multitasking and academic performance. *Computers in Human Behavior, 28*(6), 2236–2243. https://doi.org/10.1016/j.chb.2012.06.031

Kay, R.H., & Lauricella, S. (2011). Unstructured vs. structured use of laptops in higher education. *Journal of Information Technology Education, 10*. Retrieved March 18, 2019 from https://www.learntechlib.org/p/51065/

Lundquist, C., Spalding, R.J., & Eric Landrum, R. (2002). College student's thoughts about leaving the university: The impact of faculty attitudes and behaviors. *Journal of College Student Retention: Research, Theory & Practice, 4*(2), 123–133. https://doi.org/10.2190/FLAL-7AM5-Q6K3-L40P

Meyer, A., Rose, D.H., & Gordon, D. (2014). *Universal design for learning: Theory and practice.* Wakefield, MA: CAST.

Mullenax, J. & Fiorito, N. (2017). Establishing a culture that values twenty-first-century professional learning. In E. Berquist (Ed.), *UDL: Moving from exploration to integration* (55–74), Wakefield, MA: CAST.

Newton, P.M. (2015). The learning styles myth is thriving in higher education. *Frontiers in Psychology, 6*. https://doi.org/10.3389/fpsyg.2015.01908

Norris, N. (2017). Building a UDL culture: Professional learning communities. In E. Berquist (Ed.), *UDL: Moving from exploration to integration* (75–98). Wakefield, MA: CAST.

Olivia, P.F., & Gordon, W.R. (2013). *Developing the curriculum* (8th ed.). Boston, MA: Pearson.

Posey, A. (2018). *Engage the brain: How to design for learning that taps into the power of emotion.* Alexandria, VA: ASCD.

Rao, K., Ok, M., & Bryant, B. (2014). A review of research on universal design educational models. *Remedial and Special Education, 35*(3), 153–166.

Roberts, N., & Rees, M. (2014). Student use of mobile devices in university lectures. *Australasian Journal of Educational Technology, 30*(4) 415–426.

Rose, D.H., Harbour, W.S., Johnston, C.S., Daley, S.G., & Abarbanell, L. (2006). Universal design for learning in postsecondary education: Reflections on principles and their application. *Journal of Postsecondary Education and Disability, 19*(2), 135–151.

Sana, F., Weston, T., & Cepeda, N.J. (2013). Laptop multitasking hinders classroom learning for both users and nearby peers. *Computers & Education, 62,* 24-31.

Shelton, E.N. (2003). Faculty support and student retention. *Journal of Nursing Education, 42*(2), 68-76.

Tossell, C.C., Kortum, P., Shepard, C., Rahmati, A., & Zhong, L. (2015). You can lead a horse to water but you cannot make him learn: Smartphone use in higher education. *British Journal of Educational Technology, 46*(4), 713–724.

Universal Design for Learning Implementation and Research Network. (2011). Critical Elements of UDL in Instruction (Version 1.2). Lawrence, KS: Author. The original MITS Critical Elements are located at http://mits.cenmi.org/

Introducing the
CAST Skinny Books®

"Don't tell me everything. Just give me the skinny!"

Skinny Books by CAST address critical topics of education practice through brief, informative publications that emphasize practical tips and strategies. We talk about these books as "multivitamins"—densely packed with helpful knowledge in a small, digestible format.

We welcome new proposals. Got an idea? Let us know at *publishing@cast.org*.

While every Skinny Book will be in tune with the inclusive principles of Universal Design for Learning, not every title needs to address UDL specifically. For those that do, the authors may assume readers have a knowledge of UDL already.

If you need an introduction to UDL, check out our free online multimedia book *Universal Design for Learning: Theory & Practice* published at *http://udltheorypractice .cast.org*.

You can also purchase this or many other titles on UDL from *www.castpublishing.org*.